From Poppies to Ivy

A Mother's Journey during Her Son's Heroin Success Story

Karen Byers

FROM POPPIES TO IVY
A MOTHER'S JOURNEY DURING HER
SON'S HEROIN SUCCESS STORY

iUniverse books may be ordered through booksellers or by contacting:

iUniverse
1663 Liberty Drive
Bloomington, IN 47403
www.iuniverse.com
844-349-9409

Because of the dynamic nature of the Internet, any web addresses or links contained in this book may have changed since publication and may no longer be valid. The views expressed in this work are solely those of the author and do not necessarily reflect the views of the publisher, and the publisher hereby disclaims any responsibility for them.

Any people depicted in stock imagery provided by Getty Images are models, and such images are being used for illustrative purposes only.
Certain stock imagery © Getty Images.

ISBN: 978-1-6632-1025-8 (sc)
ISBN: 978-1-6632-1027-2 (hc)
ISBN: 978-1-6632-1026-5 (e)

Library of Congress Control Number: 2021908611

Print information available on the last page.

iUniverse rev. date: 06/10/2021

To my son Elliott, who has not only just worked so hard to stay clean and sober but has reached for the stars and is making his dreams come true. Thank you for the inspiration you give to me.

To my father, Grandpa Duck, who taught me the value of reading and the power of words.

To my husband, whose calm and positive support has been invaluable to both myself, while writing this memoir, and also to my son Elliott, who was able to see what being a real man is supposed to look like through your motivation and everyday living.

Contents

Preface

THIS IS MY STORY. EVERY WORD IN THIS BOOK IS TRUE EXCEPT THE NAMES AND locations, which were changed. This is what happened to me, the mother of an intelligent, precious, and talented heroin-addicted high school dropout who got clean and went on to great things. My words are derived from my experiences, from my history, and from my interpretations based on what I saw, heard, and felt during almost a decade of time.

I share my experience of the man I dated for almost a year before I discovered my son's addiction because what I saw when I was with him shaped how I reacted when the discovery was made. His son was so different from mine in every way. A person who has no experience with drug addiction pictures an addict in a certain way. There are expectations about how an addict looks and acts and smells. Those expectations are not always accurate. Perceptions are sometimes wrong.

I describe my marriage to my son's father because mental health affects so many people and can affect a family in so many ways. Self-centeredness does not have a place in a parent's life—at least it shouldn't.

I wrote this story because every time I told someone about it, that person was stunned. Some friends asked if they could share my story, and that is when I thought I must put it down in words. If my words can help one person—one mother or father who may be going through something similar—then the four years it took me to throw myself back into the nightmare and put everything into words would be worth it.

So many real-life drug addiction stories end with an overdose or a parent or person who loves an addict almost killing him- or herself with the effort it takes to save the loved one. My story is different. My story is about the addiction, recovery, and *success* achieved by my son who worked so hard to get where he is today.

I have seen other parents go through similar experiences, but they couldn't take the action I did. For whatever reason they had, they could not be the tough motherf'er I was. We are all different and shaped by our experiences. We all must find our own way.

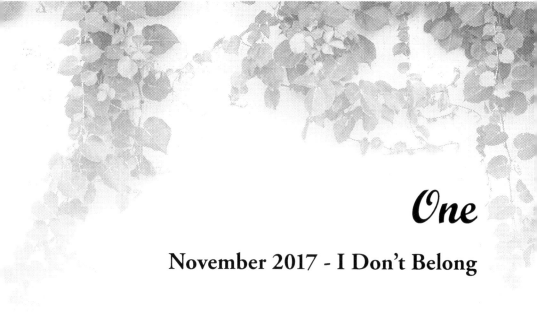

One

November 2017 - I Don't Belong

Tweet! I vaguely heard the annoying birdlike sound signaling to me that a text was coming from my phone.

I was half awake, everything in a blur between dream life and reality. I struggled to open my eyes to see the clock on my bedside table when my phone rang. My phone was set on do not disturb during this ungodly time of the night, so I felt a chilled rush through my chest as if I'd just jumped into a cold lake. Something was wrong.

I picked up my phone and heard my daughter's voice. "Mom, Elliott is talking about killing himself. I've got him on my phone texting him. He's at a bar, Mom. He's been drinking. Mom, I'm scared."

Panic struck. Melissa, my eighteen-year-old daughter, was three hundred miles away at college, and her twenty-two-year-old brother, Elliott, was in some bar in Denver drunk and talking about suicide.

Elliott had moved into my 1,500-square-foot home in Loveland, Colorado, with my fiancé, Nick, and I about three months earlier. Before that, he had been living with his father in a swank two-bedroom apartment in downtown Denver. They had lived there for only a few months when his father realized he couldn't afford the high San Francisco–like rent. Why he didn't realize that fact *before* he moved into the apartment is beyond me but not surprising, as that's the way Blake's brain worked when it came to finances. *Purchase first, and think about it later; I work hard, so I deserve it.* He could no more afford a two-bedroom apartment in Denver than he could drive his car without texting. He had rear-ended two vehicles in the past six months—both times as he was reading or sending a text.

Blake told Elliott that he found a room in a house located in Aurora, Colorado, that he was going to move into. It was Blake's chicken-shit way of telling Elliott that he didn't want him living with him anymore. Elliott had to deduce the fact that his dad was going to rent a room somewhere else, and he would have to find a place on his own. Blake's communication skills were about as good as his financial skills.

Elliott struggled with his father's lies, internalizing them to mean that his father didn't care about him or want him in his life anymore. High anxiety, paranoia, and irrational fears ran through his veins. His heart was broken and then crushed to find out his father didn't move into a room in a house but instead downsized to a one-bedroom luxury apartment closer to his on-again, off-again girlfriend and her ten-year-old son. Blake wanted his son, Elliott, out of the picture—not his life, just his living space, so he could mend his relationship with a woman who was set to inherit a huge fortune—one he would enjoy spending but could never make on his own.

Elliott was four years clean from an addiction to smoking heroin and was now taking classes at Aims Community College, holding a 4.0 grade point average. Two years earlier, he'd been a high school dropout. At this time in his life, he needed stability and support, which was imperative to stay off heroin and motivate him to continue getting straight As in college.

Blake had pulled Elliott's security rug out from underneath him. At a time when Elliott needed support and encouragement, Blake decided to throw him out on his own so Blake could spend his money on wooing his girlfriend. Pay off debt? Save for the future? Be a good father and help support your son who worked so hard to stay off heroin? Oh, hail no. Spend more than what you bring in was more Blake's way of thinking when it came to financial responsibilities.

The adrenaline from the phone call made me sit straight up in bed and command that Melissa keep Elliott communicating. Keep him on the line. Don't let him go. I kept seeing my handsome boy with the full head of thick, wavy brown hair, bushy dark eyebrows, and large blue eyes reaching up to me with his mouth wide open, trying to scream as he was sinking down into some dark abyss. But he was too far down for me to grasp his outstretched hand. Melissa sent a screenshot of Elliott's text: "I don't fit in anywhere. I don't belong here. I don't want to be here anymore."

I called Elliott, and he immediately picked up. "Hey, Mom. Sorry. I'm on my way home. Don't worry. I'm OK."

Sorry? He was apologizing for scaring me. He knew what he'd done. Was he seeking attention or sympathy seeking? Maybe.

Nick and I got out of bed and waited for Elliott to come home. Wrapped in our bathrobes and sitting in the living room, we waited until we heard a car door shut outside nearby and knew Elliott was home and walking to the front door. A wave of relief went through me. He was home. Elliott was not another statistic, and this mama wouldn't be planning a funeral.

As the front door slowly opened, I could see my Elliott with his head hung low as he was trying to be quiet. Did he actually think we had gone back to bed and fallen asleep? Kids these days comment about hating life on this earth one second and pretend nothing happened the next.

I approached Elliott and wrapped my arms around his tall, thin body.

"Sorry, Mom. I'm OK. It was just Melissa. She was exaggerating."

I told Elliott I had seen his texts, and it was not Melissa. "It's you, sweetie. You need help. You need to get back on medication and go talk to someone." It was the typical everyday motherly advice probably given a thousand times a day by most mothers—*not*. I had a therapist in mind who had helped me during a difficult time in my past—the only one of many who didn't just sit and listen to my story an hour a week for months on end but actually gave me advice on how to control the thoughts that ran through my mind and made it impossible not to cry. Elliott agreed to reach out to him.

Two

Summer of 2012 - David to First Date

ALMOST TWO YEARS AFTER I DIVORCED BLAKE AND NOT HAVING HAD ANY REAL romance for years before that, I was pushing my empty cart in Sam's Club and looking at a package of batteries—one pack with something like fifty batteries for $12.99—oh, the joy of saving money by buying in bulk. As I stood there trying to decide where I would store all these batteries, a tall, handsome older man approached me holding what I later found out was his usual drink from Sam's Club: a hot mocha. Turns out this attractive man came to Sam's Club on a regular basis. He lived just a few streets up on an acre of land with a beautiful pond and wooded area in the back.

This man, turns out, recognized me as the mother of one of his son's good friends from elementary school. I couldn't place his face or name when he gave me the overly used pickup line, "Don't I know you?"

Yes, my eyes rolled to the back of my head, but only in my mind, as I thought, *Oh, brother, that's a good one. You couldn't be more obviously trying to pick me up.*

We ended up talking for a long time, and I did remember his son, Dustin, coming over to my house when the now high school junior was in elementary school. But I didn't remember the father's face. His name was David. David followed me around Sam's Club and kept talking as if we were there shopping together but with two separate shopping carts. He finally got the nerve up to ask me to dinner sometime. I just thought to myself, *Well, this seems like a nice older and attractive man. What the hell. What do I have to lose?* So, I gave him my number, and he called me a few days later to set a day and time for this dinner date thing.

When he called, he mentioned something about Dustin recently wrecking his Mercedes and asked if I would be so kind as to drive. I agreed, and he gave me his address. Of course, it would be an address in a wooded area in Greeley where my GPS ended up sending me in circles. I finally called him on my cell phone, and he agreed to walk out to meet me.

I was driving my orange VW convertible on a dirt road with two beautiful horse pastures on either side of me. The fields were lined with freshly power-washed white fences, and numerous horses were spread out with heads lowered, chewing the grass down to its roots.

David came walking along a side road with his hands in his pockets. He was wearing jeans and a flannel shirt and kicking up dirt as he walked in his cowboy boots. *Well, that's a look I've never dated before.* He came over to the driver's side door and opened it, asking if he could drive the car. I obliged and got up to walk around to the passenger side of the car. He moved the seat back to accommodate his long legs and leaned over the middle console to open my door. So far, so good for this cowboy gentleman.

David turned the car around and headed out of the quaint country neighborhood toward the restaurant he was going to take me to. We were driving on the freeway with my long hair flying all over the place, which never bothered me like it would other women who wouldn't want to mess up their hair for anything. I remember looking over at him, and he looked back and said, "I'm going to marry you someday."

What? Who says that on a first date? Nobody had ever said that to me before. There was a part of me that thought, *How sweet*, while another part of me cringed.

Ah, but if I only knew then what I found out much later, I wouldn't have decided to take that as a compliment. I would have realized this man's head was in the sand and surely not in reality. I found out later that David kept his head in the sand on some other issues as well—issues that would later help me see something with my own son and know that I could *not* do the same.

But I thought *Well, that's a nice compliment—a bit strange, but nice*, and continued with our date. Dinner was all right, filled with the usual small talk on a first date, including filling in gaps of failed marriages and scenarios of dealing with children turning into teenagers. Of course, I had to drop him off at his house, which I later realized may have been his plan. His house was beautiful, located on an acre of landscaped property surrounded by acres of plush horse pastures and a dirt road that separated a pond with cattails and wild yellow iris flowers growing in the shallower areas.

As we pulled into the gravel circle close to the entrance of the one-story Spanish-style house, he invited me to come into his home. There was a covered patio with arched openings instead of posts and a red-tiled roof that gave it the charming Spanish flare. I agreed to come in for a bit, and we walked into the house and stepped into the open kitchen/dining/living room, which had vaulted ceilings and a large stone fireplace. It was enchanting.

He showed me around the three-bedroom home and left his master bedroom for last. He had a king-size bed made of dark wood with a large matching dresser against the wall. The room had a sliding glass door on the far wall that led to a covered deck where a hot tub was conveniently located. I looked inside and quickly stepped back toward the door, telling him that I had to leave now and thanked him for dinner. David stepped in close and leaned down, giving me a kiss. It didn't last long, as I pulled away, quickly left the house, and got into my car to leave. I was not about to be seduced by this man on the first date. Nope, not going to happen.

Three

November 2017 - That Next Morning

THAT MORNING AFTER ELLIOT HAD TEXTED HIS SISTER FROM THE BAR, I reached out for help first. A good mama who knows her child needs help rarely steps back and does nothing. I found the website of my long-lost, most helpful therapist, Dr. Michael Ross, and called the number for his office. Of course, it went to his voice mail; it was way too early to expect him to pick up the phone. I left a message. Yes, it was a bit too long, but in his line of work, that's probably a common event. I mean, what person who needs psychological help leaves a short message? The previous night's incident was briefly explained. I also let him know about Elliott's background of childhood sexual abuse and how, in my opinion, it may have resulted in Elliott's anger issues, which led to drug abuse, an addiction to heroin, and the now current concern of not wanting to be on this earth.

Michael Ross was one of those therapists who was a diamond in a coal mine. Patients would drive for hours to sit down with him for only one. His message said he was not accepting new clients, but I took the chance that because Elliot was my son and I was once his client, then maybe he would stretch his policy and take on a new patient for me. Bless my lucky stars because that was exactly how Dr. Ross looked at it too. He accepted Elliott as a patient.

When Elliot got up in the morning, I reminded him to call Dr. Ross and gave him his office number. I also reminded him to call his medical doctor to get back on medications. There was no saying no to these requests. You live in my house, you live by my rules, and my rules are to get help right now. Elliott didn't argue—didn't even put up a fight. He knew he needed help. This wasn't the first time I had noticed something wrong and jumped all over it. He knew I meant business.

Dr. Ross fit Elliot into his schedule that week.

Four

Summer 2012 - Not Until the Second Date

NOT UNTIL THE SECOND DATE … I'M NO HUSSY. I DEMAND RESPECT … RIGHT. It had been too long without the warmth of a man and that amazing feeling of skin on skin. I couldn't resist. I gave in to my carnal urges and was quite pleased with the results.

Ah, new relationships are so nice. The hidden pasts haven't been revealed yet, and there's nothing but newness and pleasure. The joys of infatuation … It didn't take long for that period to end. I soon found out that David had been engaged to a woman who lived with him for about a year. David said she broke off the engagement and left him because she wasn't comfortable with the relationship between David and his son. I wouldn't be surprised if she wasn't the first one to leave him for that reason, as she sure wasn't the last.

We were three weeks into our new relationship when David revealed something about Dustin that I later found out wasn't quite the truth. The truth was horrific—something nobody would want to be a part of or have in their lives. David wanted to keep me as far away from the truth as possible to keep me close to him.

Dustin was David's son and had been Elliott's best friend in elementary school. They were both little goofballs when they played together eight to ten years before I dated David. They were loud and very active when they got together at my house. Both had extremely creative little brains, thinking up imaginative fighting ninja games and running around the house and backyard screaming as they held up their pretend weapons ready to attack an approaching made-up monster or villain.

In Loveland, all neighborhoods had a piece of property designated for water runoff thanks to all that glorious rain in the spring. Those lots would hold the excess water and were perfect homes for frogs. Elliott and Dustin would frequent those frog-infested lots and bring home some of the population. This frog-collecting, frog-racing, frog-torturing endeavor would create hours of fun-filled after-school, weekend, and summertime playdates. *Playdates* is what us parents would call those get-togethers … Sounds stupid now when I look back on it.

Five

Autumn of 2000 - Neighbors Visit

Our neighbors had four boys. Karl was the oldest, but he was off to college by the time they moved into the house on the west side of ours. The next oldest son was Gerald. Gerald was the same age as my oldest son, Brandon. The next two were Paul and Ryan. Paul was sweet, and Ryan was hyper. Both boys had their own special learning issues. Paul appeared slow but had a heart the size of an ox, I always felt nothing but pure love coming out of that boy. Ryan, however, was nothing like Paul. He had an infinite amount of energy and had difficulty getting his words out. When he talked, it always seemed like he had just run eleven miles as fast as he could and was completely out of breath.

I mention these neighbors because I believe Elliott's issues began in their house when Elliott was around the age of five. It was during a weekend when his oldest brother was at his dad's house. Elliott asked if he could go over to the neighbors' house to play. At the time, I loved these neighbors. They were a good, church-going family with kind and special sons who I thought were perfectly harmless. However, nothing was ever the same after that day. My sweet boy who adored his little baby sister and helped his mama every chance he could experienced something inside that house that changed him forever. That one incident changed his innocent, trusting little self and turned it upside down. Ever since Elliott was a baby, people would stop me to tell me simply how beautiful he was. I, of course, would smile and thank them for the compliment and let them know I couldn't agree more. He was my Campbell's soup baby. He looked just like that baby face on the soup can, and his I'll-take-care-of-this-mom attitude made him just as beautiful on the inside.

Elliott went to the neighbors' house and was only there for a few hours when he came back home with the angriest demeanor I've ever observed in him. I asked him, "Hey, sweetie. Did you have fun?"

Immediately, I got his reply. "No!" He couldn't look at me and instead stomped his feet on the kitchen floor and ran upstairs to his bedroom.

Well that's odd, I thought as I laid my dish rag over the kitchen sink faucet and started following him up the stairs to his bedroom. "Honey, what's wrong? What happened?"

"*Nothing!* Nothing happened! I don't want to talk about it!" That was when his bedroom door became a blur as it flashed toward my face and stopped fractions of an inch away from flattening my nose as it closed shut.

Take a deep breath, everything's fine, I told myself as I put my hand on his bedroom doorknob and began turning it. Slowly, I opened the door and peered my head around, part of me thinking I was about to get something thrown at me, when I saw my Elliott facedown on his bed. I was thinking to myself that Paul or Ryan must have said something mean to Elliott. I was expecting to hear some story about one of them telling Elliott that he was stupid, or maybe one of them picked his nose and, like lots of boys do, chased him around with the boog at the tip of his finger threatening to wipe it on him or, worse, did wipe it on him.

But Elliott wouldn't talk no matter how hard I pried or how many different questions I asked. So, I thought I'd wait for him to come to me. For days, he would go about his day doing the same things he usually did but with his head down low, quiet, and angry.

Six

Summer 2012 - As Far as I Knew—Secrets

As far as I knew, Elliott and Dustin just grew apart, and each hung out with a different group of friends. There was no big fight that happened between them.

Elliott was now a junior in hgh school and participating in the Running Start program at Aims Community College. Aims CC was a nationally ranked community college that participated in a high school program called Running Start. This was a program where high school students would get tested, and if they scored well enough on these tests, they could get accepted into the program where they would leave their high school campus and take college courses at a participating community college. Some students would graduate from high school with an associate degree. Talk about saving on tuition costs.

Elliott was also heavily involved with the high school drama program. In ninth grade, Elliott asked to be enrolled in YAPI at a local acting company that would put on plays using local actors and actresses. YAPI stood for Young Actors Performing Intensely. It was an all-day camp-like program held in the summer where the kids would learn all the ins and outs of acting, and it would end with a trip to New York City where the kids attended several Broadway productions and met some of the actors and actresses in those productions backstage.

David's son, Dustin, was doing nothing like that. Dustin was going to school and coming home to his room located in the opposite end of the house to play video games or watch television. David believed he was doing his homework diligently and being an average teenager making his way through his high school years with all the typical issues involving classes, the SAT, girlfriends, and prom or homecoming. Oh, but Dustin was doing anything but the typical things that a high schooler does.

I first realized this when Dustin continuously asked David for money—not large amounts, just a few bucks to get some lunch or dinner here and there and quite often. David never held back, always opening his wallet and handing Dustin several dollars. He must have been thinking this is what a good father would do. Dustin didn't live with his mom. His mom was a recovering alcoholic. Her alcoholism was what ended David's marriage with her. She and Dustin just didn't get along, and Dustin needed his father now that he was getting older. That's how I interpreted what I was being told. It's how my brain interpreted what I was hearing from their conversations and David's explanations to me when an argument between the two of them would erupt.

There was a night when I was at David's house, sitting on the couch watching television when Dustin came in again for what seemed like the hundredth time in a week asking for ten dollars. David got upset for the first time in front of me and appeared exasperated when he reached into his back pocket to pull out his wallet and handed Dustin another ten-dollar bill. That was when Dustin commented that he was going to get some Suboxone from a friend and assured his father that everything was under control.

That night I found out the quasi truth about Dustin. Dustin had an addiction, and a doctor had prescribed a medication by the name of Suboxone. Ah, the quick-fix drug Suboxone. Dustin assured his dad that he no longer needed a doctor and was treating himself with Suboxone that he could buy on the street. This was my first street-drug experience of any kind. I was stunned at what I heard. David tried to explain that Dustin had been treated by a physician about a year ago and was put on the medication Suboxone to help with his addiction, but he stopped seeing the doctor and was now using Suboxone to treat himself.

David's words were spinning in my head as I was trying to make sense of what he was telling me.

Seven

Autumn 2000 - What Happened at the Neighbor's House

It wasn't until a few days later that I learned about what happened at the neighbors' house. I was outside kneeling on the ground pulling weeds in my front yard flower garden when he walked up to me. I saw his cute little red and white gym shoes standing by the dirt I was working in. I looked up at him and met his beautiful big eyes. He had his baseball hat on his head and his baseball glove on his left hand. I could tell he wanted to practice his catches and throws.

"Want to play?" Elliott asked me, holding out his ball.

"Sure. Let's go to the backyard where there's more room," I replied.

I stood up from being on my hands and knees and started following Elliott as he led the way around the house to the backyard. "So, what happened the other day Elliott?"

Elliott's walking slowed and became more of a foot dragging. After a few minutes, he started talking. "It was Gerald. I hate him. He took me in his room and closed the door … I couldn't get out!" The anger was seething and intense.

"Where were Ryan and Paul?" I asked him.

"I don't know. They were probably in their room" Elliot said. Elliott was again looking down at the ground and swinging his arms. He was nervous, and there was another emotion I was trying to put my finger on … He was ashamed.

Something had happened in Gerald's room—something that made my sweet, happy boy become an angry, quiet little person. I knew this was serious. Something in a mother's heart just knows by listening and watching her children when something horrible has happened, and this moment was telling me everything I needed to know. I asked Elliott if we could go talk with his father about this.

Blake was inside working on one of his many projects. In those days, projects for Blake were used every weekend as a way to get out of doing mundane work like pulling weeds, mowing the grass, doing laundry, washing the dishes, cleaning the bathrooms, you know, the typical chores that are supposed to be split equally between two working adults. No, Blake would create unnecessary projects that he could work on around the house and spend ridiculous amounts of money on tools and materials and even more time going to Home Depot over and over and over again.

Melissa was born the year before and was still a handful, especially when it came to weekends and doing mundane chores. I'll never forget that wrung-out feeling when I would work full time at the office Monday through Friday only to wait for the weekend when I would work all day Saturday and Sunday doing the usual chores around the house and taking care of the kids while Blake kept himself busy with his unnecessary projects. Did we really need that wall shelving unit between the fireplace and wet bar, which was really used as the guinea pig cage counter? That shelving project took more than six months. Three times it had to be completely torn apart and started over due to what he called *mismeasuring*. Isn't there a motto for construction? Measure once and check twice?

I interrupted Blake from his project and told him something happened to Elliott involving Gerald, and we should all talk about it. Blake and I did our best to remain calm and question Elliott in a way that would not make him any madder than he already was. We wanted to find out exactly what happened behind those closed doors. We had to be very specific with our questions. "Did he pull your pants down? Did he pull his pants down? Did he touch your penis? Did he put his penis anywhere near your bum?"

Elliott answered no to all our questions. He told us that Gerald had brought him in his room, closed the door, and made him turn away from him. Gerald then rubbed his hard penis against Elliott's backside. That's all we could get out of him. To this day, I'm still not sure what really happened and if Elliott, because this happened at such a tender age, could be capable of telling us.

Anytime I was outside in the front yard with Elliott and Gerald would come out of his house or arrive home, Elliott would run inside and be furious with the world. He would run up to his room and start throwing things against his wall.

Within a week after Elliott's revelation that Gerald did something to him, I scheduled an appointment with his pediatrician, who gave us a referral to a child psychologist nearby. I'll never forget the first appointment we had with the pediatric therapist gentleman. His name escapes me, but his face never will. It was a misshapen face, but there were no scars, so it couldn't have been from an accident. It was difficult for me to look at him with one side of his face being almost twice as long as the other. If it was hard for me to look at him, I can't imagine how a child suffering from any kind of post-traumatic stress disorder or sexual abuse would feel. He told us he would start out by playing games with Elliott and try to get Elliott to open up to him.

After several sessions and no improvement with Elliott's anger, we stopped the sessions. Elliott hated going and said he couldn't stand the games and stupid talk with the deformed-faced man.

Eight

Autumn 2012 - When You Are in the Stage of Infatuation

WHEN YOU ARE IN THE STAGE OF INFATUATION AND THE FIRST NEGATIVE THING happens, you immediately want to discount the bad and focus on the good. *No, no, no, I'm not hearing this right*, I thought. *Something doesn't make sense here.*

David had a nonchalant attitude where he acted like it was no big deal—this was a normal, everyday thing that happens to all families. It convinced me at first. My problem was that I'm an honest person, and I don't downplay anything … I am blunt and say it like it is. "Deal with it" was my motto. If I'm dealing with someone who may not be truthful or isn't being straight with me, I tend to believe that person initially. I listen to the person with the expectation that he or she is giving me the truth.

As an insurance claims consultant, I learned, however, that you can't and shouldn't trust everything that people tell you. Some people want something from you. Some people want to hide something from you in order to benefit for themselves. After my initial trust started to wear off, in a day or so, I started thinking about what David told me and what I saw with his interactions and dealings with Dustin's constant requests for money. I began rehearsing in my mind what he told me about the Suboxone and doctor's treatment. Why would a parent allow his child to treat himself for something he had been under a doctor's care for in the past? Why would a parent allow his child to purchase a medication from a street supplier or a friend? It just wasn't adding up in my brain and my heart.

I knew I needed to talk to David about his shady explanations. But again, taking skills from my job, I did my own investigation behind the scenes. I did a search on my computer for Suboxone and found numerous sites explaining the most common use of this medication was for the treatment of an addiction to opioids—oxycontin and heroin.

Heroin. The word was out there, and fear crept in. Immediately, visions of dirty, skinny, sweaty people came into my head. Those people would be holding out their bent arms and poking themselves with a syringe with the other shaking hand. Once the needle was pulled out of the vein, I envisioned the addict, usually an unbathed, shirtless man, lean his head back with his mouth wide open in sheer relief and ecstasy.

That was when the curtain of infatuation closed on the stage of my relationship with David. I was no longer feeling that nice, warm, fuzzy feeling that this man I'd found was perfect. Oh no, far from perfect ... *Maybe I should walk now and cut my losses*, I thought. But he was so nice and such a giving man. For the first time in years, I felt like someone wanted to take care of me instead of the other way around, which was my failed marriage to Blake.

I drove over to David's house with the pure intention of talking about this pit in my gut. Too bad for David, I wasn't the sweep-things-under-the-rug kind of gal. I walked to the door, feeling the knots in my stomach doubling and tripling inside and my hands getting cold and clammy. I hated confrontation but knew that it was necessary to have an honest relationship and to be able to live with myself. In order to have a confrontation, I needed to believe I was valuable and deserved to be heard.

David opened the door, and I stepped inside. His house was warm and comforting. He wrapped his arms around me as he welcomed me inside. My face pressed into his clean-smelling shirt, and I dreaded the conversation I was about to have. It would be so much easier to just forget it—just pretend it wasn't there and look past the obvious.

Within seconds, I pulled away and told him that he hadn't been honest with me. I asked him if Dustin was using Suboxone for an opioid addiction. David's head dropped, his shoulders slumped down, and he couldn't look at me. He didn't respond. I asked him if Dustin was using heroin. David nodded his head yes and turned away from me. He was ashamed. He was embarrassed. He was scared—scared that I would not want to be involved with a man whose son was a heroin addict. He tried to assure me that he believed Dustin and that he was getting better and no longer using heroin but instead taking Suboxone, which, in his words, was "so much better."

"Dustin is a great kid," he said, trying to convince me. "Dustin is so smart," he said. "Dustin did a lot of research and is doing exactly what his doctor was doing when he was seeing the doctor. Dustin's got this ... He'll be fine."

David then asked me for my forgiveness. He loved me and didn't want to lose me. Everything would be OK. He promised.

Nine

Years 2001 to 2008 - Hockey to Help the Anger

WHAT ELSE COULD WE DO FOR ELLIOTT TO HELP RELIEVE HIS ANGER? HOCKEY was our answer. Blake played hockey growing up and was a competitive skier, and I was a high-level competitive gymnast, so with his father and mother both being athletes, it appeared Elliott got the same genes. Oh, and hockey worked wonders for Elliott. He was a natural athlete and took to skating like it was second nature.

He started in peewee and almost immediately became a star. He was a fast little skater and could shoot pucks into the net with unbelievable ease. For years, he kept his hair shoulder-length, and it poked out from under his helmet. I could always spot him when he was on the ice; all I had to do was look for the hair whizzing around like a speed demon. His teammates' families would cheer his name when he would skate by and so often get the puck into the net for a goal. He made good friends with his teammates, and the coaches loved him.

Elliott loved hockey and still does. It wasn't until it got to the stage when checking was introduced that I noticed some hesitation. I would look into his big brown eyes and see his trepidation before a game. His mouth would open and close as his tongue would touch his top lip showing how nervous he was. Those eyes were telling me that Elliott did not like getting hit, and his soft heart did not like hitting other players.

But he continued to play, learning the right technique to flatten another player and the right way to avoid getting squished like a bug. Did the techniques always work? No, but the knowledge and Elliott's skill set helped him stay in the game, and with his help, his team continued winning games. We used to go to every game, but after several years, Elliott made it on a select team. He became so good that he was often traveling, and we couldn't make it to every game anymore.

We would get calls from the coaches about possible concussions or fractures, and they no longer made my heart jump—that's how often they came in.

Elliott and his team were traveling to Canada, Chicago, and LA. Pretty soon, we were just dropping him off at the rink where a travel bus would be there for the team to take to their next destination where a hockey game or tournament was scheduled.

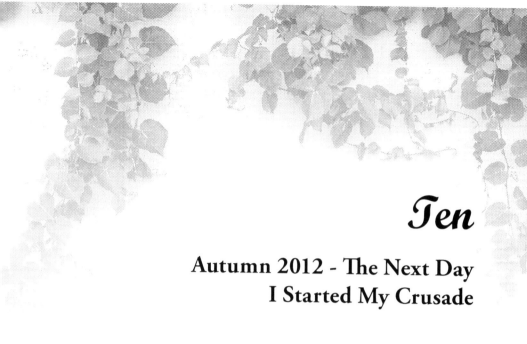

Ten

Autumn 2012 - The Next Day
I Started My Crusade

DAVID'S PLAN OF HOLDING BACK THE TRUTH SO THAT MAYBE THIS GIRL—*ME*— would fall in love with him and stay once the truth came out worked. The next day, I started my crusade to find out everything I could about suboxone and heroin addiction, so I could help my man deal with his son—the son who was my son's best friend in elementary school, the tall, good-looking, sandy-blond kid who used to run around my house with my Elliott playing with our dogs and the frogs they collected.

David also had two other children. The oldest daughter who was strikingly beautiful and extremely skinny with an obvious eating disorder, which was later confirmed. Her name was Ashton. She had an adorable son named Adam. I fell in love with both of them, but Adam was my sweetie. In no time, he called me grandma. I had this beautiful bundle of little boy energy and love in my life who innocently called me Grandma! He had dark blond hair and inquisitive brown eyes. He loved wrestling and running around the house and yard pretending that I was Monster Grandma running after him to gobble him up. When I caught him, I would wrap my arms around his stocky little body and bury my face in his tummy as I made grumbling noises like a monster chewing on her prey. He would giggle until he could barely breathe, and we would collapse on the ground afterward only to have him jump on top of me begging for more.

David also had another daughter whom I never met. All I knew about her was that she was in a very expensive design college that David was paying for, and she preferred girls. OK, so he had an oldest daughter with an eating disorder, a middle daughter who was a talented artist and lesbian, and a son who was treating himself with street-bought Suboxone for a heroin addiction—just the kind of family I wanted to join.

I soon found myself listening to the requests Dustin was making to David for money. and the reasons he was giving for needing the money became more and more absurd. There was a time we were sitting on the couch watching television. It was dark outside, and David had a fire going in the fireplace. We had made ourselves a little "party," which was a plate of meat, cheese, crackers, and vegetables. and we each had a beer to wash it all down with.

Dustin walked in the room and asked his dad for forty dollars for spring prom. It was October. David pulled out his wallet and handed him the money. I softly told David that spring prom wasn't for another five or six months. It was as if a light bulb went off in David's head. *Oh, hey, she's got a point there!* Or maybe he was just pretending. I'll never know. But I do know that it took me questioning David's constant and instant reaction of pulling out his wallet and giving in to every request Dustin made for him to stop and start questioning Dustin and his motives.

David's questioning would make Dustin irritable. He would beg and plead and give reason upon ridiculous reason for needing the money, and then if David didn't give in, he would erupt in anger. He would call David every name in the book. He would throw anything he could get his hands on and yell at the top of his lungs how much he hated David.

David was an electrician, now retired and teaching at the Greeley Technical College. He wasn't used to having to deal with such negative and combative behavior in anyone, let alone his own son. It was horrible, and it was starting to become an everyday occurrence.

Eleven

Year 2005 to 2010 - Melissa and Gymnastics

AROUND THE TIME WHEN ELLIOTT'S HOCKEY TRAVEL WAS RAMPING UP, MELISSA started the competitive sport of gymnastics. Our family seemed to naturally split, with me taking Melissa to the gym and Blake taking Elliot to the rink. I had been a pre-elite gymnast when I was younger and was in the gym six days a week training or teaching six to seven hours a day in the summer. During my junior year of high school, I was getting out of school early to walk to the bus stop and ride two buses to the gym every day. Gymnastics was my life when I was growing up, and now that I was a mom, I loved watching my daughter learn new skills and routines.

I almost became one of those crazy moms who communicates with her child from the stands. I found myself in the viewing area with my laptop working in the gym and sneaking peeks at my daughter and telling her how to fix her body so she could get a skill. "Keep your head back, Melissa … Point your toes … Arms up Melissa-Moo!"

I realized I was on my way to becoming one of those moms I could barely tolerate. I knew I had to do something to put an end to it, so I asked the owner of the gym if I could coach. How could they say no? I was asking if I could teach beginning gymnastics and the first year of competition level. Most of the coaches they had teaching those levels were young teenagers who were actively using their cell phones on the gym floor and were busy texting when they were supposed to be teaching. Those young girls trying to teach gymnastics obviously didn't know what they were doing, I think I was the best thing to happen to that gym. OK, maybe not the best thing, but I was good for the gym, as more and more kids were signing up for my classes and parents were constantly giving the gym compliments on how I motivated their kids and made them feel good about themselves.

Coaching gymnastics became my new passion. I loved it. I relished how these beautiful little girls loved my quirky personality and would run onto the floor when it was time for class to begin and shower me with hugs. I loved making each one of them feel special because they were.

We put on a mock meet at the beginning of the season where the girls would perform for their families and other coaches would be the judges. Everyone got a medal. I took on the role of the coach who made the girls see how fun the sport of gymnastics could truly be.

After several years, Melissa was at a higher level, and the coaches at that level weren't as qualified as I felt Melissa needed. It was at the end of the year, and the co-owner coach had a meeting with us. He told us that Melissa was talented, and if we wanted her to get to a high level of gymnastics, then we should take her to another gym. We started looking, and I found a new gym close by. I spoke to the head coach at the new gym, and she agreed to let Melissa try their gym to see if she liked it. She didn't give me a coaching job but said that if things worked out for Melissa, she would consider hiring me for their first year of competitive team.

My world was Melissa's gymnastics and my coaching. Elliott was in such a high level of hockey that we were now just dropping him off at the rink where he would practice or get on a bus to a tournament in Canada, California, Oregon, or Montana.

For me, it was a relief to be somewhere I felt valued. Blake was so wrapped up in his self-created anxiety or irrational fears that it was nice to be away from his high-level emotional roller coaster—emotions that he demanded everyone in the family be a part of or else he thought we didn't care about him.

Initially, I never thought of divorcing Blake. I had already been married once before; I was *not* going to get divorced again. That was simply out of the question. I could be happy with my passion of coaching, my kids, and my job. I could love the good parts of Blake and continue that way for the rest of my life … or so I thought.

Twelve

C's

I CONTINUED TO STUDY HEROIN ADDICTION, THE USE OF SUBOXONE (WHICH IS also addictive), the signs of drug use, what parents do to help a child who is addicted, and what a parent can do to make things worse. There are the three C's of addiction that emphasized:

1. I did not *cause* this.
2. I cannot *control* this.
3. I cannot *cure* this.

But there's one more *C* that is involved that a parent *can* do for an addict that is harmful and that is: *contribute*. David was a contributor. He contributed to his son's addiction by giving his son everything his son wanted. David did not put down boundaries in his household and stick to them, making his son follow David's rules. Enforcement was something David was not strong enough to do.

I read hundreds of blogs written by other parents going through the experience of having a child addicted to a drug. It was heartbreaking to read their stories and feel the pain they must be going through watching the child they raised and love being swallowed up by the DOC (drug of choice). There were hours upon hours of time reading articles about Suboxone and how-to articles about helping a loved one get clean.

There were also articles about addiction to Suboxone. Some articles referred to Suboxone as the drug to help get off a worse drug, but they noted it was still addictive, just not as bad as the other drug: heroin.

Thirteen

Years 1996 to 2009 - Failing Marriage

SOON, I FOUND THAT BLAKE WAS ALWAYS LOOKING FOR SOMETHING TO GET INTO a fight about. He was never happy and had something to be sad or upset about every single day. It was exhausting; he was extremely high maintenance. I found myself longing to just have him be happy. *Just give me one day where he was happy,* I thought to myself.

I'll never forget a time when we were in the kitchen. He was upset again about something at work, and I sighed in exasperation. Blake asked me why I would sigh, and I told him, "You have something to complain about or be negative about every single day." He argued with me, and I pulled out the calendar where I'd written down every complaint he'd had for the last month. I showed it to him and started reading his issues and what they were every day for the past four weeks. That shut him up for the day ... but it started back up in a few days.

He also constantly needed something expensive to fill some kind of hole in his psyche.

When we first got married, he needed a $3,000 computer to look for a job after I told him that I was not going to be taking care of him as he flitted from part-time job to part-time job looking for what made him the happiest while I worked day in and day out to pay the bills and pay off his debt. I made it very clear to Blake that with a baby coming and day care expenses on the horizon, he needed to get a real full-time job. Maybe that's when Blake became resentful. Maybe he just wanted a mom-wife: a wife who would take care of him like a mom. I soon realized he needed a strong woman who would take care of him and his numerous issues with his anxiety, irrational fears, and physical ailments. Blake wasn't a grown man and never will be; he was a permanent boy who needed his mommy.

Soon after we moved, Blake's mommy moved too. She moved to Loveland, Colorado. His mommy bought a place five minutes away from our house. His mommy would walk right into our house, unannounced. His mommy was always there helping her poor little Blake. With me and his mother, Hannah, Blake had two mommies to help him with his many crazy ailments. Of course, I didn't realize this until years into our marriage.

Blake also needed to satisfy his sex drive, and that's when I wasn't his mommy. However, Blake's sex drive was incapable of being satisfied. One-on-one sex wasn't enough for him; he needed more than that, and he wanted me to play along.

He brought pornographic videos into our marriage within the first few months. He had to have ripsnorting sex-capades, which were fun and different at first, but then he wanted to make the fantasies into reality. He wanted to watch me having sex with another woman, another man, or maybe get involved with many people at the same time. I didn't mind the fantasies; what two consensual people do behind closed doors is their business. That's how I looked at it, but for me, it had to stay in the fantasy world—the world where you closed your eyes and imagined yourself in it.

Blake wanted to take pictures of me and videos of us in the act. He assured me that just taking the provocative pictures and videos was a turn-on for him, and he would never do anything else with them. There was just one problem. I hadn't figured out by then that Blake was a habitual liar. I later found out from snooping on his computer one day that Blake was a member of a website for swingers and was using the photos he took of me and communicating with other swingers as if I were sitting next to him as he was emailing them about meeting and hooking up.

I found this website on his computer history and read the communications between Blake and other swingers. I was mortified and considered separating at that time. Blake's excuse was that it was a turn-on for him to read people's reactions to my pictures, and he felt lucky to have me. *Uh, thanks?* I kept the documentation for years while I considered using his actions as a reason for divorce.

Five years later for our ten-year anniversary he took me to Vancouver, Canada, and as a surprise to me, we met with a couple who was interested in swinging with us. Blake hadn't stopped his escapades in hopes of making his fantasies a reality with me. I felt sick to my stomach and completely vulnerable, as if I were naked, but it was all happening in a dark Vancouver restaurant with all of us fully clothed.

The couple was attractive and nice, but I was shaking the entire time—shaking with anger that Blake was putting me through this, especially on our anniversary weekend, and shaking at the fact that this was actually happening. Maybe I should have gotten mad, thrown my drink in Blake's face, and stomped off. No worries, though, the fantasy did not come to life to my relief (and I'm sure Blake's disappointment), we left the restaurant with the couple saying they would get in touch, but thank God they never did. They probably sensed my anger and knew I wasn't into the idea of getting down and dirty with them. After that, I'd had enough. I flat-out told Blake that if swinging was something he really wanted, then he should just divorce me now because I was never going to make it a reality.

Blake never stopped his pornography habit, however, and I soon found him sleeping in front of his computer at night with his head hanging down, chin resting on his chest, drool dripping down his shirt with his hands in his pants, and his favorite porn website still running. The level of respect I had for this man was dipping into the negative. It's one thing for a wife to find her husband in post-having-sex-with-himself sleep with his favorite pornography instead of her, but it's a whole other completely enraging thing when a mother finds out that her son or daughter also found him the same way ...

Fourteen

December 2012 - Christmas Party

CHRISTMAS WAS JUST A FEW WEEKS AWAY. I HELPED DAVID DECORATE HIS house. It was our first Christmas together. We went to one of the many Christmas tree farms close by. There was a large red barn with the rounded roof and miles of nicely trimmed trees; any of them would make the perfect Christmas tree. Families were scattered throughout with the dad or older brother holding the saw, ready to claim the prized tree. Holiday music was playing, and hot chocolate was being served. There was even a Santa sitting inside the gift shop with a line of kids waiting to sit in his lap and tell him what they wanted to find under the tree on Christmas morning.

David and I found a beautiful tree and cut it down. We purchased it and had it go through the shaking machine to remove all the loose or dead needles. It was then wrapped up and secured in the back of his truck, and we brought it back to his house.

The rest of the day was spent decorating the tree. Hundreds of lights were strung along the branches, garland was hung, and bows were attached to each of the top rungs of the garland. Colorful shiny balls and ornaments were hung on the tree with Christmas music playing.

We were in such a festive mood that we decided to have a holiday party and invite our friends. I brought over a few boxes of my holiday decorations to his house. Lord knows I have a few to spare! We splashed Christmas cheer all over the place. Lights were strung all along the top of his house and along the arches on his porch. Santa Claus figurines were splattered throughout the house. There wasn't a corner of the room without something Christmas in it. It was truly transformed into a magical Christmas house. I love the holidays.

The night of the party, we loaded all kinds of food and desserts on top of the kitchen island. David had a warm fire going in the fireplace, and the lights were on outside and on the fully decorated Christmas tree in the corner of the large family/kitchen/dining room. Our guests started piling in. I was happy. I love the holidays, and any reason to get together with friends—to eat, drink, hang out, and get dressed up—is right up there on the top of my list. The house was full. My daughter was there with a friend, and my son Brandon was there talking with David's oldest daughter. They appeared to be flirting. Christmas music was blaring, and people were laughing. It was everything a good holiday party could be.

Until the sliding glass door opened, and in came Dustin and his friend Jeffrey. They were glassy-eyed and stumbling. Dustin was saying something, but I was too far away from him to hear over the blaring Christmas music. David immediately rushed to Dustin, took him by the arm, and led him out of the family room with Jeffrey following.

My best friend Adam was there with his husband Mark. Mark was visibly upset. He had been standing close to the sliding glass door when Dustin and Jeffrey opened it, and he must have heard, smelled, and seen things I hadn't because he wouldn't stop exclaiming how *devilish* and *evil* both Dustin and Jeffrey appeared to him. It's funny. When you're not around something a lot and it is suddenly pushed in front of your face, you notice it differently than if you saw it every day … I was seeing it every day. Had I grown numb to it? It didn't hit me that hard—not like it did Mark. Mark was a well-educated and successful chiropractor. He came from an affluent family, and seeing Dustin and Jeffrey in the state of being high out of their minds was something Mark didn't see very often. To him, it stuck out like a sore thumb.

When David came back, he heard Mark talking about his disgust for what he just witnessed. Mark was concerned for me and my safety. He didn't want me in this house with this creature … this monster, as he saw him. "He wasn't talking coherently, and his eyes were black, evil. That kid was pure evil. You can't be around this, Karen."

Adam and Mark are not your typical gay married couple. They do not dress flamboyantly, as a straight person might imagine a gay man dressing in feminine soft fabrics and pastel colors. They were the opposite; in fact, they were constantly hit on by women when they went out to bars or even on airplanes while flying to their various properties. Adam was often mistaken for the tall handsome, country singer Blake Shelton, and Mark was just as good-looking. They both had a lot of masculine ruggedness that many women found attractive, and apparently, many men did too. I didn't care either way. I loved them like family.

We tried to resume the party and bring back that joyous shimmering holiday feel, but the spell had been broken. The room was no longer sparkling with glee. Instead, it became somber and almost dark. Our guests gradually began leaving and wishing us well.

Merry Christmas! Happy holidays! Don't forget the dark little spider in the back of the room … It's lurking, ready at any moment to jump out into reality and sink its fangs into your skin as its venom oozes into your blood.

Fifteen

Years 1996 to 2009 - Husband with Extreme Anxiety and Irrational Fears

It wasn't just Blake's sexual issues that caused problems with our marriage. His ultra-anxiety and fear of the unknown or ridiculous was also a huge factor. He was always afraid of something bad happening. It felt like he would require that everyone around him be just as anxious and just as wrapped up in his anxieties and fears as he was.

One of his regulars was his fear that he would lose his job. Like a restaurant customer who came in for a meal every week, that fear would come into our lives every few months. Blake would become consumed with his certainty that he was going to be fired or laid off. Fear would ooze out of his pores as he walked through the door after work. His head would hang low, and he would start talking in his high-pressured businesslike voice while throwing his briefcase on the kitchen floor. The kids would look up from whatever they were doing and get a scared look on their faces. Their eyes would widen and start watering with concern as they bit their bottom lips. *What is Daddy going to do? Why is Daddy so angry?*

I would be the reassuring but scared and nervous wife consoling her husband as he was ranting around the house. I was the wife telling her husband that everything was going to be OK and that she made enough money to keep the family afloat for a while until he got another job.

"Breathe, darling. Breathe," I would tell him. "Kids, go to your rooms and play. I'll let you know when dinner is ready."

Sometimes Blake would be so upset he would be close to crying, which would engulf me with fear and anxiety for what may happen to my dear family's life. We would stay up at night for hours talking through things as if the worst-case scenario would be happening and what our plan would be. It was draining. I believe Blake needed to go through all of this to ease his fear. If he knew that

I could take care of everything if the worst thing happened, then he didn't have to be scared.

The clincher was when a few months would pass, and Blake's employment performance review would come along. He would get a raise with flying colors and compliments. How could this happen? Wasn't he about to be fired? That's when I began to realize I married a crazy man who was consumed with his own extreme anxiety and needed constant reassurance.

There was a time when Blake had some digestive issues that put him in the hospital. He was released after a few days and diagnosed with diverticulitis with the possibility of Crohn's disease. He was a mess with anxiety about what could be happening with his body.

The kids and I were in the family room when Blake started his anxiety rant. His voice would raise in pitch and volume. My stomach would tighten with the anticipation of what was about to come … and it came. In front of the kids, as I was trying to calm the ranting man-child, Blake yelled, "I'm afraid I have colon cancer!"

The kids were startled with fear of their dad dying. They both began to cry and ran to their dad, clinging to his legs. Seeing my children's reaction started a vise-grip feeling in my chest. I was livid with anger. It's OK to have those fears and relay them to another adult in a one-on-one conversation, but to put those fears on small children who don't understand that it's just a fearful thought, not reality—that was cruel. I grabbed Blake by the arm and forcefully led him up the stairs to our room after peeling our crying children off his legs.

Again, I was Blake's mother calming him down and getting mad at him for saying something like that in front of our children. My momma-bear instinct took over. I found myself feeling like I had to protect my cubs from this psychotic baby. That's what Blake was becoming to me: an idiotic, crazy predator who was harming my children with his anxious rants and raves over his numerous stupid everyday fears.

Sixteen

December 2012 - Dustin's Girlfriend's Christmas Gift

A COUPLE OF DAYS AFTER THE HUMILIATING CHRISTMAS PARTY IT WAS ALL about Dustin getting a gift for his beloved girlfriend, Chelsea. The Christmas party ordeal was swept under the rug. David refused to believe that Dustin and Jeffrey were high as kites. It didn't matter how much Mark ranted in revulsion; David objected to such crazy talk. Dustin was fine. He wasn't wasted; he was just tired—drained from all the gaming he and his friends were doing in the back room and exasperated from all the Christmas shopping he just did.

Of course, Dustin needed money for Chelsea's gift, and he wanted to get her something nice. They had been dating now for almost a year, and she was the love of his life. David went with Dustin and picked out a ring with semiprecious stones. I was watching television and waiting for them to return when the door from the garage flew open, and David and Dustin came walking in. They were happy, laughing, and smiling like a father and son should be who just spent quality time Christmas shopping together. David was excited to show me what Dustin picked out for Chelsea. He pulled out the tiny red velvet box from the bag and opened it to show me. The ring was beautiful, and David was so proud that he was helping his son make his girlfriend happy with such a nice gift.

I think back on it now and have no doubt that the ring was exchanged for pennies on the dollar, by either Dustin or Chelsea, who was also an active heroin addict. The exchange was for more heroin or cash for more heroin. Either way, David's unselfish festive mood just helped his son and his son's girlfriend gain access to more heroin. It was indirect, but just the same, the addict was being a master manipulator.

Seventeen

Spring 2010 - Meeting with My Husband's Therapist

BLAKE HAD NO PROBLEM GETTING INTO FIGHTS WITH ME IN FRONT OF OUR children. I would plead with him to remain calm and explain that we could talk about his issues later when the kids were in bed. It didn't matter how hard I pleaded with him, he would never heed my requests to stay quiet and calm—not around the children. His anger would always rise to a level where we would both be yelling at each other with our children watching, pulling them into our intense drama.

It wasn't just Blake's anxiety that hurt our children; that was a somewhat hidden and passive-aggressive harm. Blake was also perfectly capable of making the hurt obvious and physical. There were numerous times he would lose his patience with the kids and physically hurt them. He would pick up Elliott and throw him in his room in a fit of rage and spank him hard. He would do the same to Melissa. Numerous times, I got in his face, pointed my finger at him, and threatened to take the kids and leave if he ever did it again. The problem was, where would I go? The house was mine. I had paid for it with the sale of my house, which he had no ownership of. I paid off his debt. He was the best one to leave the house, as he could just go five minutes away and stay with his mother. No doubt she would gladly take him in and take care of him.

Blake started seeing a therapist. I wasn't sure why and I didn't really care, as this seemed like a common occurrence. Blake was one of those on-again, off-again patients with numerous therapists. His father was a psychologist. I believe in psychologists and the fact that mental health is real and can be treated. It wasn't like I didn't support him seeing a therapist. Maybe it was just another exhausting melodramatic move Blake was making that would turn out to be nothing. I was tired. This routine of sympathy- or attention-seeking behavior was making me feel like a wrung-out rag. Blake asked if I would go with him to his therapist.

I agreed to go to Blake's therapist, but the intense caring about why he was going or why he wanted me to go wasn't there. God, I was exhausted. Blake started talking. He told me that this time he was seeing a therapist because he was having urges and desires to have an affair. As I sat in our first session listening to Blake talk about his fears and concerns with our marriage, something snapped inside. I couldn't do this anymore. I had lost all respect for this man years ago and couldn't take his anxiety and extreme fear of the unknown any longer. I asked the therapist if I could meet with her by myself. Blake looked startled, and I saw fear in his eyes.

"What? Why?" he asked.

I didn't answer right away. I didn't care. I was numb—numb from the mental torture he put me through for years. Emotions were high and intense, needing to find solutions to the pretend scenarios that never came to fruition. I had to get out.

The next week I met with her and told her I couldn't do this any longer. I told her the things Blake had done that caused me to completely lose all respect: the extreme anxiety that flooded our home when Blake had his daily outbursts and the childish behavior from Blake when he couldn't control his irrational fears and wanted every family member to sink into those same fears and support him or he would die. I told her that I wanted her help. I wanted to tell Blake that I wanted a divorce during a therapy session with her. I felt like she would protect me. Maybe Blake wouldn't blow up and be totally irrational with her in the room.

Eighteen

January 2013 - Ugly Spider in the Corner

DAVID TOLD ME THAT BEFORE HE BUMPED INTO ME AT SAM'S CLUB THAT HE was engaged to a woman who left him because of his relationship with Dustin. She told him it was dysfunctional, and I was starting to see how right she was. I didn't want to break up with this kind man. Life seemed so perfect if we could take away the one problem: Dustin. After I spoke with my oldest son, Brandon, about the situation and asked for his advice, he told me, "Mom, you have a nice man who lives on this beautiful piece of property in a beautiful home, but with Dustin there, it's like you have an ugly brown dirty spider in the corner always lurking." Brandon was a wise man, full of experience and suffering of his own.

Dustin didn't just have a heroin addiction problem; he also had a hygiene problem. His neck was always caked with dirt. David would tell me that he didn't understand why Dustin wouldn't wash himself. I would often hear David telling Dustin, "Hey, go take a shower and wash your neck. It's filthy."

Whenever I was at their home, Dustin was either out with friends or in his room with the door shut playing video games. Dustin was constantly complaining of being in excruciating pain because he was not able to have a bowel movement. If he ever did, it was an epic event, as he experienced extreme pain and the size of his dump was enormous. Dustin would get David and show him the size of the dropping—I mean, dumping—still lurking in the toilet and tell him the great discomfort it caused him. David believed there had to be something medically wrong with him; this just wasn't normal. David took Dustin to the doctor several times, and they would tell Dustin to bathe more and prescribed stool softener, but nothing seemed to work.

One night I was watching the nightly news when a television commercial came on that grabbed my attention and woke me up from what felt like a strange dream. Have you ever noticed how there are a ton of medication commercials on during the news? This one was about opioid-induced constipation and medication that can be used to treat it. The commercial described how opioid pain-reducing medication can sometimes cause constipation, which can make a person uncomfortable and interfere with the enjoyment of life … hmmmm. A light bulb went on and a loud *ding* went off in my brain, Dustin was suffering from opioid induced constipation—of course! It all made sense.

Nineteen

Spring 2010 - Failed Marriage

THIS WASN'T THE FIRST TIME BLAKE HAD GONE TO A THERAPIST; HE HAD BEEN seeing therapists all his life. His father was a medical doctor turned psychiatrist. Blake was constantly calling his father with his anxiety issues and irrational fears. His father was, in turn, constantly recommending different medications for him. When I first met Blake, he was on medication. After I thought I was in love with him, I naively asked him to get off the medication, so I could get to know who he really was. He naively agreed, and after a few months of experiencing my nonmedicated Blake, I told him—no, I begged him—to get back on the medication.

Blake's comments that he wanted to see a therapist this time because he started having feelings that he wanted to have an affair and thought it would be wrong was crap. Oh, please. I knew that Blake had already had an affair a few years earlier. He was working at Oracle, and her name was Amber. Amber was a young blonde girl who took a fancy to Blake. Blake was quite the charmer when he wanted to be. Blake was good-looking and gave the impression that he was intelligent, so, of course, he would attract someone similar. He got me, didn't he?

He had *me* fooled is what he did! I was pregnant when I married Blake and felt that I owed it to my unborn baby to try my best with his father, so he could have a normal life. I should've gone with my gut feeling and bore the judgmental stares and criticism from the old-fashioned world. I'll never forget Blake's reaction when I told him that I was pregnant: "I don't want to be just a weekend dad." It was that statement that made me feel like I *had* to try a marriage with this man. But it was this same man who picked his first fight with me four months after saying our vows. The topic of this fight—one that turned into many—was that I trapped him into marrying me.

I trapped him, as if I wanted to get pregnant and by *his* sperm. And what a catch he was with $50,000 in student loan debt, creditors calling asking why he hadn't sent payments from numerous credit cards, an $8,000 loan for medical treatment when he broke both ankles in a rock-climbing accident, and two part-time jobs, one as an adjunct professor at Spencer College and another as a quality control engineer at Rough Cliff rock-climbing gear company. Blake saw himself as a catch, and I trapped him. *Ha!* I had graduated from college and had a full-time job with Allstate Insurance that provided a 401(k), a pension, and good benefits. I owned a house and drove a Mercedes. Blake was delusional, but that wouldn't be the first time his crazy would show its ugly face.

Twenty

Years 2012 to 2013 - Comparing the Two

DUSTIN WENT TO THE SAME SCHOOL AS ELLIOTT. DUSTIN, HOWEVER, WAS NOT in the Running Start program. Dustin was barely passing. Dustin was missing assignments, not going to classes, and failing tests. Dustin wasn't employed, making the excuse up that he was applying but nobody was hiring.

Every other week or so the school attendance office would call David and let him know that Dustin wasn't in school that day or Dustin missed several classes or Dustin was behind in his assignments.

"What? How could this be? Dustin is a good student," David would say to me if the calls came in while I was with him. "He's a smart kid!"

In the meantime, Elliott got a job at a Relax the Back furniture store and was getting the lead roles in the high school drama and musical productions. He was on the high school improv team, and they had just won the Hogan Cup, a statewide high school competition held in downtown Denver. The kids were quick on their feet and funny, and Elliott was a star. Elliott was also on the presidential honor roll at Aims Community College (as a high school student), and his confidence was soaring. I was so proud. Elliott was nothing like Dustin. Elliott was involved, got out of the house, performed on stage, and was on the presidential honor roll at a community college. As a mother, I couldn't' be prouder.

Elliott took showers and washed his neck and behind his ears, unlike Dustin. Elliott dressed well and always seemed to be in a good mood. Elliott was funny and mesmerizing on stage. He was charming. I went to all his performances. Every time Elliott was on stage my attention would zoom to him. But, of course, it would; I'm his mother! I was there to see my son and nobody else, so of course my focus would go directly on Elliott when he was in my sight.

When Elliott would play his role, I became absorbed in his character as if he were no longer my Elliott. Instead, he was the person he won the audition to be. There was no awkwardness when I watched Elliott, unlike some of the other so-called actors on stage. Those so-called actors would hesitate before their lines, and their nerves would erupt with the shaking in their voices. Elliott's voice was clear, audible, and precisely on time with emotions that made you believe he was no longer inside his own body but taking on the persona of another person. Oh, but I saw that and felt that because I was his mother. A mother would love even the ugliest baby, right? But after every performance, other mothers would approach me and introduce themselves as one of the mothers of a so-called actor who dripped with awkwardness and nerves while on stage. Those mothers would grab my arm or shoulder and lean in to tell me how good Elliott was: "He is such a natural up there on stage. It's definitely his forte!" *So, it's not just me?* I remember thinking. *Others feel the same way?* Yes, my Elliott was good; he was going places …

Sometimes it was like I was living two lives: one with David and his loser, heroin-addicted son, Dustin, who was failing in school and life, and the other as the mother of three beautiful kids. My oldest, Brandon, was living in Austin, Texas, and paying his bills with his bartending job while he was trying to make it in the music scene. He graduated from college and was now making it on his own. My oldest was out of the nest.

There was my middle son, Elliott, who was on the presidential honor roll at Aims Community College while in high school and was a brilliant actor and comedian. Then I had my adorable daughter, Melissa, who was a beautiful gymnast with legs like Olympic gold medalist Nastia Liuken which appeared to be able to bend backward. Melissa was working out at the same gym where I was coaching. I was proud of my kids, who were all doing well and were basically happy.

Twenty-one

Spring 2013 - F'ing Kill You

ONE MORNING WHEN ELLIOTT AND MELISSA WERE WITH THEIR DAD AND I spent the night at David's, we were woken up by Dustin knocking on the bedroom door. David got out of bed, threw his robe on, and left the room to see what Dustin needed. Surprise, surprise ... Dustin needed money. An argument erupted. Dustin yelled at David that he needed lunch money. I could hear David calmly telling Dustin to make himself lunch with the food he bought in the fridge. That wouldn't work for Dustin, and he yelled at David that he didn't have time. Dustin became so angry he began yelling at the top of his lungs. Profanity was flying out of both mouths.

I had snuck out of bed and put my robe on but stayed just outside the door. I wanted to hear what these two were saying. Dustin must have been by the front door, which was closer to the bedroom door from what I could hear, and I'll never forget hearing him say under his breath but loud enough for me to catch it: "I hate you! I'm going to fucking kill you!" And then I heard the front door open and slam shut. The sound of tires moving fast on the gravel driveway as rocks were spit onto the side of the house was all I could hear after that until it was silent.

David came back in the room as if it was just another lovely sunny morning. I had gone back to bed but was sitting up with the covers up to my chin quivering inside. I never did feel comfortable with conflict, but that scenario frightened me. I told David what I heard Dustin say under his breath. David didn't believe me—or probably didn't want to believe me—but he told me that he would talk to Dustin about it later that night.

I later found out that when David talked with Dustin about what he said, Dustin denied saying any such thing. Of course he did. He wouldn't want his father, who put a roof over his head and gave him money for his heroin habit, to know that he wanted to kill him when he didn't give him money. I knew differently. I read the blogs where parents of heroin-addicted children were threatened by those children when the parents got tough and refused to give them money. I knew what was going on.

Unfortunately, David refused to do the work. He refused to read the blogs. He refused to study the effects of heroin. He refused to open his eyes to what was happening right in front of him. In his mind, Dustin was fine, he was a smart kid, and he had everything under control.

Twenty-two

Spring 2013 - Engaged

IT WAS SPRINGTIME, AND NEW LIFE WAS POPPING UP EVERYWHERE. THE SOIL showed new plants struggling up between clods of dirt to get their share of the much-needed sunshine and warmth. The trees were showing buds opening with new leaves and flowers. Just outside my back door my favorite bush was sending out shots of sweet smells that filled my nose with the taste of Sweet Tarts. New life was all around. God, I loved this time of year!

David planned a weekend away. He rented a little cabin, and I could tell there was something special he was planning. He was very creative planning our time together whether it was a picnic of exotic fruit, homemade sandwiches, cheeses, special desserts, and never-before tasted beer on the beach; hiking in a national park with a stay in a rustic lodge; or taking the kayaks out to a small lake we'd never been to. The man was always thinking about doing something new with me, but this time was different. He seemed nervous, and his daughter called more often than usual. I knew it was coming … He was going to propose. He was such a sweet man, and we had so much fun together … but there was that spider in the dark corner.

The drive to the small resort was beautiful. Tall evergreen trees lined the roads, and every couple of miles there would be an opening with a small home and swing set, showing a family was living their lives in this gorgeous setting, so remote and rustic and far away from the fast suburb life I was immersed in.

Once we got to the resort—if that's what you want to call it—we got out of the car and stretched our legs. I reached up to the sky to pull up the muscles in my shoulders that felt tight and cramped from the car ride. The resort had several small cabins on about an acre of land. There was a main house with a welcome sign: "Come on in. We are open and baking cookies!" Seriously, they offered freshly baked chocolate chip cookies—the kind that when you broke them in half the chocolate would string from each half and then drip down … delicious!

There were five other small cabins on the property, each with its own theme. We stayed in the nautical cabin. There were small model ships on shelves, a wooden ship steering wheel hung on the door in the place where a wreath would be, and boat anchors tied with rope were scattered throughout. There was even a towel ring in the bathroom made from industrial pipe rope. Hundreds of seashells were scattered about in every nook and corner.

This was a two-room cabin. There was the main room with a small kitchenette, a two-seater dining room set, and a king-size bed. What set this room apart was a big hot tub placed smack-dab in the middle. This room was all about romance. The second room was a private bathroom. It was special, all right—not like the last lodge room we stayed at with the ceilings so low we had to duck to get into the bed and into the tub.

I was nervous. I knew David was going to pop the question, but when and how was he going to do it? I didn't want him to know I was onto him and knew what he was up to.

We took a walk around the resort and outside around the town. The quaint town was on a bluff, and we walked across the street to an opening between buildings. I wouldn't call it a park, but there were a few benches by the edge with a spectacular view of the valley below and a picnic table. Was it now? Was he going to get down on one knee and ask me to marry him in this sort-of park?

Nope. We sat on the bench and relaxed as we gazed out at the beautiful valley. David put his arm around my shoulders. I closed my eyes and inhaled the smells of the new spring blossoms and David's aftershave. I heard the songbirds, and every once in a while, I heard a car slowly drive by. The sun was out, making the temperature warm and comfortable.

After about a half an hour, we both felt hungry and decided to look for a restaurant along the main street for a bite to eat. Hand in hand, we walked along the sidewalk until we came to a building that had a restaurant upstairs. The menu was on the wall next to the door, so we skimmed through the choices and prices. The specialty was Easter Bunny (it was almost Easter) with Brussel sprout puree, spring vegetables, and a long-grain wild rice medley. Sounded good to me—I'd heard rabbit tastes like chicken. We opened the door and walked up the narrow and steep staircase to the restaurant. *Could this be the place? Is he going to pull out a small box with a ring inside and ask me to spend the rest of my life with him?* Nope. We sat at a table by a window that looked across the main street and out on the ocean but no proposal.

After dinner, we walked back to our quaint little cabin with the ships, shells, and anchors and climbed into that king-size bed. The next morning, we had breakfast delivered to the front door, which had come with the price of the cabin. We were eating fresh avocado and cheese omelets with fried potatoes and rosemary toast. That was when David asked me to marry him. He was sweet and shy about it. He looked me in the eye and told me I was the best thing that had ever happened to him. He said he couldn't live without me and that I would make him the happiest man on earth if I married him. I wrapped my arms around him and said yes. Then he pulled out the little box with the little ring that had the little diamond. Yes, I emphasized that word ... Everything about it was little. I was surprised at the smallness of the diamond, but that's not what mattered. He told me that I could pick out my own ring. This was just a ring to fit the occasion ... little? I wasn't exactly sure what he meant by that ... Was the engagement little?

His last fiancée had broken off the engagement, and he probably didn't want the same thing to happen. Maybe he lost money on that ring. I put the ring on my finger and thought it was beautiful. Really small, maybe a quarter of a carat ... OK, it looked like a ring that a boy from high school would give to his pregnant girlfriend—let's be honest here. But I wasn't shallow and was going to wear it with pride.

Twenty-three

November 2013 - I Found the Stash

"Mom, if I told you, you would never look at me the same again."

"Tell me what, Elliott? What are you talking about?" I was sitting on the couch in the family room with the television on and complaining about Dustin's drug habits and what a loser he was. God, I hated that kid. If I didn't say those exact words, I'm sure the sentiment came through in whatever I said.

With his head down, he walked out of the room saying he couldn't say any more. "Never mind."

I got up off the couch and followed him to his room, but he had already shut the door. "Never mind, Mom. It's nothing."

Bullshit it was nothing. I saw hurt in his big blue eyes. I saw what appeared to be guilt. He was trying to tell me something. But what could be wrong? Elliott was amazing! He was now a senior in high school and still on the presidential honor roll at Aims Community College; he was voted captain of the improv team; he was co-captain of the drama club and had leading roles in the school plays; he had a sweet and beautiful girlfriend; and he had a part-time job. What else could a mother want? I was so proud of him, and he knew that. But there was this nagging little feeling in the center of my chest. What if Elliott was in trouble? Why would he say that I'd never look at him the same way at the same time I was talking dirt about Dustin? I knew what I had to do.

I waited until he left the house. "Going to rehearsals, Mom," he announced. "I will be back around 10:30."

I heard the front door shut, and then seconds later the sound of his beater SUV drove off. I walked down the hall to his room. I opened the door, and it smelled like him—like the way his head smelled when I gave him a hug if we were sitting on the couch. His room was small; there was barely a few feet between the sides of his queen-size bed and the walls. I started snooping—it's what mothers have a natural talent for. We snoop to find anything out of the ordinary. It didn't take me long; I went directly to his nightstand and started rummaging through it. I found a small leopard-print bag. I pried open the drawstring top and found pieces of foil with burn marks. I found an empty clear shell of a pen and a lighter. *WTF is this?* I wondered.

I took it out of his room and held it close to me. I walked down the hall and into my bedroom. I laid down on my bed and waited for him to come home.

I drifted off to sleep only to be startled awake by Elliott knocking on my bedroom door. "Come on in," I shouted. I was still dressed and lying on the top of my bed when Elliott opened the door. I held up the leopard-print bag, "Whose is this? Is it Angie's? Are you hiding it for her?"

"No, Mom. It's mine."

It all started making sense now—the little hints he had been giving to me over the past few months all came rolling into me like a ball of fire. This was too easy. He wasn't hiding this from me anymore. He knew he needed help. He *wanted* me to find it. I asked him what it was for just so I could hear him tell me.

"It's for smoking heroin, Mom."

I felt a blow in my chest like I'd just been struck by a sledgehammer right to the heart. My heart wasn't breaking. It was being smashed to smithereens. I could barely breathe, and the room started spinning. I closed my eyes to make it stop. I felt sick to my stomach.

Elliott was still standing there in my bedroom doorway, looking at me with an imploring stare. I looked in his eyes, and he seemed to be waiting for a reaction, like he wanted me to blow up at him and be super angry.

He then said, "Do you hate me?"

I got up from the bed and walked over to him. I reached up and put my arms around his tall, skinny body and hugged him. "No, Elliott. I love you. I'm going to get you help. We need to tell your dad."

Twenty-four

Spring 2013 - Night Before the Cruise—Ultimatum

THERE WAS A NIGHT IN FEBRUARY—THE SAME NIGHT BEFORE DAVID AND I WERE going to go on a cruise to Mexico—when Dustin woke us up by knocking on the bedroom door. David had been denying that there was a problem. David would say that Dustin wasn't using anymore and had everything under control and that the constipation must have been from his diet. He said he wasn't giving him enough money to get him any drugs, only enough for a meal at Subway, and was buying more groceries so Dustin would have to make his own meals.

David got up, and I followed. We both threw on our robes. David motioned to me with his hand to stay back. I took it that he wanted to take care of this and wanted me to stay in the bedroom. I stood on the other side of the door again as David left the room. I heard Dustin tell David that he was right. He was still using heroin, and he just needed some money to go buy some Suboxone. He could take care of this problem himself.

David came back into the bedroom and walked over to the dresser where he left his wallet.

I told David, "No, don't do it. Let's take him to a detox center and then send him to a rehabilitation facility so he could get some help. I'll help you. Please!"

David wouldn't listen. He didn't want to fight with his son. David grabbed his wallet from his nightstand and left the room. He gave Dustin money instead. Dustin was a master manipulator, and David was the master enabler. It was the perfect combination for a complete waste of a good life and a lifelong addiction.

My breath escaped me as I watched David pull out money from his wallet. I wanted to leave—just walk out on all this crazy. But I'd bought the plane tickets and the cruise, and David had bought the activities during the cruise. I wanted to go to Mexico, damn it.

We left on the cruise the next day, but I knew I had to do something serious to try to shake these two out of this sick pattern. After the cruise, I told David that Dustin had to be treated and clean or out of the house by the end of school. My ultimatum was that if David didn't comply, then I would be gone. I offered to help in any way I could.

Twenty-five

November 2013 - Doctor Appointment

THE MONDAY AFTER WE FOUND OUT THAT ELLIOTT WAS USING HEROIN, WE GOT him in to see his doctor. We didn't know where to turn and felt a medical doctor would be the best way to start to get help. Blake, Elliott, and I were in Lake Loveland Family Medicine clinic waiting for Dr. James Ranjet. Dr. Ranjet was one of those fast-talking, get-you-in-and-out practitioners. He was a straight shooter, tell-it-like-it-is kind of guy. Blake, Elliott, and I were called in by the nurse who led us to a small treatment room. It was sterile and cold. There was a picture of a small child petting a dog on the wall. Blake stood, I took a seat in one of the available chairs, and Elliott sat on the exam table.

The door opened, and Dr. Ranjet came in. He was a small man and obviously from India with his brown skin, black hair, and thick Indian accent. He was wearing his white doctor's coat and holding a notebook to write on. He shook my and Blake's hands, introducing himself and looking straight into our eyes. His hand was warm, and it felt like he was looking into my soul when I looked into his big brown eyes. After the introduction pleasantries, if that's what you want to call it, he turned to Elliott and immediately started asking him questions. "What drugs have you been using?"

Elliott told Dr. Ranjet that he mostly had been smoking heroin but had never injected it.

"What else have you been using? Anything else besides heroin in the past few years?"

That's when Elliott began listing off the names of drugs he had used. He had started smoking marijuana in junior high school. He had got it from Blake's stash hidden in his tool shed in the garage. Such great news to hear coming from my son's mouth. I felt like I was having an out-of-body experience listening to this. I knew Blake would smoke pot sometimes. I never liked it and could always tell when he had taken a few puffs. He couldn't open his eyes all the way—it was a sign he couldn't hide. But did I know he kept a *stash*? No. Lucky for him, we were already divorced, and this was no time for blame.

Elliott continued to talk to Dr. Ranjet and listed illicit drug names that I had never heard before. I was flat-out stunned. Dr. Ranjet then said something to Elliott that will never leave me.

"You are an addict," he stated. "You will always be an addict. You will always struggle with this disease."

Elliott just sat there, looked down, and nodded his head in agreement.

I felt the blood drain from my head. I thought I was going to pass out or throw up right there all over the clinic's floor. *How could this be?* I wondered. *Is this really happening? Oh, God, make this stop. Make this go away. Make me wake up from this nightmare.*

Dr. Ranjet contacted a rehabilitation service center in Glendale, Colorado, and they had an opening for Elliott. We could bring him on Wednesday of that same week. Elliott seemed open to it; he knew he needed help and was willing to do what his father and I told him. Drug use was unacceptable, and heroin use was unthinkable and unbelievably not allowed in our lives. That was what we all agreed with. Who wouldn't?

Twenty-six

Years 2012 to 2013 - Jeffrey

DAVID AND DUSTIN PUT ON A GOOD SHOW FOR SEVERAL MONTHS. DUSTIN WAS smart. He must have planned his requests to David for money when I wasn't around to help David question his requests and figure out that his requests were not real but manipulations to get money for his addiction habit. David kept telling me that Dustin was doing great. Dustin was doing well in school and set up to graduate the following year, he would tell me. However, the school continued to call to let David know that Dustin was failing classes and absent from many or, most of the time, all of his classes. David would have to go into the school to meet with the principal, Becki Sherman.

Periodically, David would have Melissa and Elliott come over to his house. Melissa and I would take the kayaks out to the pond if it was just her, or we would take walks out in the woods.

I thought Elliott and Dustin would hang out when Elliott came over, but that didn't happen. Dustin was cold to Elliott and might greet him with a "hey" and quick nod of the head and then leave and go to the dark corner of the house where he hung out and played video games. Elliott didn't react well to this. I got the feeling he thought Dustin would welcome him into the fold of the household, and they would go back to his room and hang out. Instead, the feeling I had was that Dustin felt he was too good for Elliot. I could tell that Elliott felt rejected. There went the idea of a Brady-Bunch-like combined family.

Elliot no longer considered Dustin a friend. Oddly enough, they had a mutual friend whose name was Jeffrey. Elliott would talk about Jeffrey all the time. I had the impression that he was his closest friend. Dustin would also talk about Jeffrey. He and Jeffrey were going out to dinner, or he and Jeffrey were going out to a movie. When I was at David's home, I heard Dustin talk a lot about him. At home, Elliott talked a lot about him. How could these two boys, Elliot and Dustin, who were best friends in elementary school, dislike each other but both be super close to the same kid? What was it about him that they were each drawn to but could no longer be friends themselves?

When I was at David's house, there were many times when Jeffrey would come over to pick up Dustin. He would rarely stay long and would avoid looking at me. But when I did catch his eye, they were always glassy, and he looked nervous. He was a tall, lanky kid with dark hair, dark eyes, and dark circles under his eyes. But he was funny, always making a quick remark that would crack up whomever he was with in laughter. Maybe this was what Dustin and Elliott both found so appealing with this mutual friend. But something didn't make sense. Why weren't they all hanging out together? I didn't mind because I knew Dustin was using heroin, and Jeffrey probably was too. But why didn't they get a long? What happened?

Twenty-seven

November/December 2013 - Rehab One

WE HAD ONE DAY TO GET ELLIOTT'S STUFF TO TAKE TO HIS FIRST REHABILITATION.
Calls were made to insurance companies and the rehab facility. A list of what Elliott could bring with him was given to us. Shopping was done to get the items on the list for Elliott to be as comfortable as he could at a drug rehabilitation center. Before I knew it, Wednesday morning was on me, and we were packing the car with Elliott's stuff and Elliott. Elliott looked sick and was quiet; his body was starting to go through withdrawals.

The somber drive took us about an hour. When we reached the facility, I pulled into the parking lot and parked next to a large shrub. It was dark and raining lightly. We all walked into the lobby, and I went to the window to sign in. Several other parents were in the lobby waiting. There were makeshift holiday decorations on tables and the front desk window shelf. I looked into the large window and saw a few desks and a woman sitting in front of me. She smiled and pleasantly asked if she could help me. I told her my name and that I was here with Elliot. She asked me to sign in and take a seat. I signed the sheet she handed to me, and we all took a seat. There was a girl with several piercings and tattoos sitting next to me and caught my eye. She smiled and then looked down. We all knew why we were here.

This facility was for adults and minors, with two separate quarters for each. We were soon greeted by a man who opened the door from the lobby to the heart of the building where Elliott would be living for the next thity days. He looked into the lobby and called out Elliott's name. He shook our hands and introduced himself before welcoming us to follow him through the door and into the white-walled hallways. As we walked through the sterile halls, we passed the entrance to the adult section, and the door opened as a staff member walked in. I couldn't help myself from looking inside like a voyeur, unable to look away like a good girl should. I saw some of the adult residents and felt sick to my stomach. The people I saw were men who resembled prisoners, and some of them probably were. I thought to myself, *They were here to go through detox and then a rehabilitation program before going to prison to serve time for whatever heinous crime they committed.*

Those inmates were way too close to my son for my comfort but what choice did I have? This was the facility recommended by Dr. Ranjet.

We continued through the halls, passing office doors decorated with wrapping paper and tinsel. We entered the office of Elliott's future counselor during his stay there. He had us sit and wait as he went through all of Elliott's personal belongings, checking for paraphernalia, drugs, and weapons of any kind. He found nothing, so it was time for goodbyes. My stomach felt like it was full of ice, and I was about to barf those cubes all over the floor. *This isn't happening,* I thought to myself. *I'm dropping off my son in a facility with ex-cons just a few feet away. I'm dropping off my son at a drug rehabilitation center for his heroin addiction … unbelievable.*

Twenty-eight

Summer 2013 - Neighbor with a Gun

It was a beautiful sunny day. David and I slept in, and then he made a delicious breakfast of avocado and cheese omelets, toast, and seasoned fried potato chunks. We walked outside and sat down on the log bench located on the side of the dirt road that ran between the two ponded areas. Sitting on the bench, we could look out to the deeper pond and wooded area with the sun on our backs. If we turned around, we would be seeing the other smaller pond with the horse pasture that usually contained three to four lazy and beautiful horses with their heads down as they grazed on grass. There were cattails and yellow irises along the shallower parts and dragonflies flitting around. Red-winged blackbirds were singing their mating songs. As we sat on the log bench soaking up the warm sun and listening to the relaxing sound of the birds in the background, we noticed a young man walking toward us. His head was down as he briskly walked closer. He was determined with something on his mind. I had never met him before, but David recognized him as the oldest son of his neighbor who lived to the north of him.

David stood up to greet the young man, but the young man motioned for David to sit back down. I immediately saw the gun sitting in its holster on his hip and the young man's hand on it. I didn't feel afraid but could feel fear in the young man standing in front of us.

I greeted him with a hello, and he gave me a cold look then immediately started talking directly to David. The fear and anger in his voice was prevalent as he told David what he saw happening in front of his house at night. This was *his* neighborhood, and he would not tolerate this any longer. He described seeing Dustin with packages and exchanging the packages for envelopes of what he could only guess was money. He had no doubt, and he made it noticeably clear, that he knew what was inside those packages.

"I will *not* tolerate drug dealing in my neighborhood," the man snapped. "I have taken videos and photos of this bullshit and will take them to the police if I have to."

David stood up and apologized to this young man and told him he would do something about it right away. I stood up with him and followed him to the house. The young man turned around and walked back toward his house. I then realized that this young man was wearing a gun because he himself was afraid of confronting David. I now believe it took everything this young man had inside of him to talk with David. He probably felt like he had to do what he could to stop this madness from happening in his quiet, affluent neighborhood in the country—a place where drug dealing should never be happenng. That happens in dirty, crowded cities, not here, not where horses graze and life feels relaxed and slowed down to a comfortable pace.

As David was walking toward the front door, I pulled on his arm to slow him down. Everything I had been telling him that he had refused to believe and that he would not accept was truly happening was now being confirmed by a neighbor who had witnessed it. There were so many times I told David to get Dustin help and stop believing Dustin and the excuses he continually gave. David refused to believe me because it was so much easier to believe his son. It was so much easier to believe that his son was doing fine—sweep reality under the rug, stick your head in the sand, close your eyes, and don't look at it. Reality of drug addiction with your child is too difficult to deal with for many parents. It's so much easier to pretend that it's not there. David believed there was nothing you could do about it. An addict had to *want* to stop on his or her own. You just had to patiently wait until the person was ready—that's what David believed.

David would use the Alcoholics Anonymous mentality and say to himself and to me, "No amount of help will work if an addict doesn't want it to work." He explained that he went through this with his ex-wife. She had to *want* to stop drinking before anything would help her. He felt the same way about Dustin and heroin. Dustin had to *want* to stop using before he would allow anything to help him. David was just waiting for Dustin to be ready.

I pulled David to a stop and made him face me. I could tell his mind was reeling. He was just given a bomb that basically blew up in his face in front of me ... Dustin wasn't just still using heroin; he was also dealing it, and his neighbors all knew it. David didn't deal with conflict very well; he obviously didn't deal with reality very well either. I asked him how he was going to deal with this. He just looked at me ... I could tell he didn't know what to say. After a few seconds that felt like hours, he told me he was going to go talk with Dustin. My heart sank. *Here we go again—all talk and no action.* I thought to myself. *This conversation will be Dustin talking his way out of these accusations and convincing his father that they weren't true.* I stressed to David how important it was to *not* believe what Dustin was telling him and to actually take some action this time.

He had limited time. I gave him until July to get Dustin out of the house, or I was gone. If David wouldn't force Dustin to go into detox and then a long rehab so he could get the tools to help himself, which was what I continued to suggest to him, then he had to make Dustin leave the house. I would not stay and watch this game any longer. I went through it myself with Elliott and was willing to help David. I would support him if he would do it my way. But David believed that Dustin had to come to the realization that he needed help on his own.

David was afraid. He asked me, "What if Dustin stops loving me? What if I desert him, and he gets so angry with me he stops loving me?"

Is that what parents of child addicts think? I didn't. I just thought about doing everything I could to get him to stop using. Who cares how he felt or what he said at the time? It's not really the addict talking or acting out anyway; it's the heroin monster that has invaded the body.

Twenty-nine

December 2013 - Al-Anon Meetings

WE WERE ADVISED BY THE REHABILITATION CENTER TO GO TO AL-ANON meetings. They told us we would need support from other parents who were experiencing the same thing. Blake and I would go and bring Melissa so she could meet separately with other siblings of drug-addicted family members. We walked into a church meeting room where coffee and light pastries were on a table in a help-yourself style. There were twenty to thrity other adults in the large church basement with chairs on one end and the table with coffee and pastries on the other end. The adults all looked normal—like us. They appeared to be hard-working, middle-class parents who were suffering. Soon, we were called to sit in a circle where the leader would start talking. Introductions were made, and then the sharing would begin.

A couple were in the circle who started talking about their son who they just found out was selling marijuana. They found a wad of money in his room. He wasn't smoking it, they said, just selling it, but they were distraught about it. I sat there listening, not being judgmental. *Thank you, marijuana-selling-son-mom. Thank you for sharing, next …*

It went on and on until I couldn't stand it any longer. Meeting after meeting, I couldn't stand hearing the stories. There were stories but no solutions. I wanted solutions. These meetings were about support. Parents sharing their stories, so they didn't feel alone in this horrible mess. I didn't want support. I wanted action. I wanted solutions. I wanted answers. Tell me this is going to get better. Tell me what I need to do to make this all get better.

Thirty

Summer 2013 - Breakup— Concert—Drop Me Off Forever

IT WAS JULY, AND DUSTIN WAS STILL LIVING IN DAVID'S HOUSE. I GATHERED THE little bit of stuff I had at David's place one morning and left. He didn't think anything of it and truly believed I was just going to my house for a bit. He didn't think I was actually gone for good ... even though I told him before I left that this was it. Dustin was still using and still living in his home, so I was done—done with this David.

The next week David called me. He wanted to know if I was still going with him to the country music concert at Red Rocks. The Red Rocks Amphitheater was a beautiful, open, natural arena where the acoustics were amazing. There were no chairs. People brought their own or just blankets and would sit on the blankets on the hill. Several concert goers would camp nearby. David reserved a hotel room for us in a nearby town. The room had been reserved for months. I agreed to go but warned David that we were not back together. I was just being selfish and wanted to see some of my favorite country music artists. To this day I don't regret going. David was a nice man, and I still cared about him. We had fun together and shared the same taste in music, so what the hell.

We had a good time. Some songs struck my heart, and I found myself crying as I knew I would never do this again with David and had no idea what was in store for me and my love life after this. I'd thought I found my forever, but there needs to be more than just a good man. There needs to be strength in that man, or at least the willingness to let me help him help his son. I could help him ... if he let me.

After the three-day weekend full of amazing music, we drove home. It took three hours to get to David's house from Red Rocks. I told him that I wanted my kayak back at my house. He looked confused and hurt. I was firm and told him to get my kayak from the side of his house and put it in his truck and follow me home. He did what he was told, like a good puppy.

When we got home and unloaded the kayak, he took me in his arms and gave me a big, long hug. By then, I was done, and the hug just made me sick. I pulled away and said goodbye. He sighed and slouched as if I had just made a joke and he didn't believe me. I told him I meant it and walked inside my house, locking the door behind me. After about ten minutes, he finaly backed his truck out of my driveway and drove away.

Thirty-one

December 2012 - Drama—Drop Out of Lead Role of Dream Play

ELLIOTT WAS CO-CAPTAIN OF THE DRAMA CLUB. GRETA STALWART WAS Elliott's drama teacher and the person he referred to as his second mom. As a senior, Elliott was given lead roles in the high school productions. Greta had chosen Elliott to be the lead role for the winter high school production. The play she chose was almost a one-man show that would emphasize Elliott's humor and extreme depth for acting. It was a dream role for Elliott—one he had wanted to perform for so long. He started talking about it a year before it was chosen. He was trying to sway Greta to choose this play and give him the lead. He knew he could shine on stage and bring the character to life. When Greta chose the play, he was ecstatic. When he auditioned for the lead, he killed it. Nobody else came close.

The day after we took Elliott to his first rehab, I had to tell Greta. She really was like Elliott's second mom. She loved him and knew how mesmerizing he was on stage. Elliott had been with her for almost three years. Drama and improv were Elliott's only high school experiences after he started the Running Start program, and Greta was his only high school teacher. She chose this play for Elliott to perform his final and best performance of his high school career. She and he both knew he was going to blow this play up beyond expectations … However, it was not meant to be. The role would have to go to someone else. I tried telling Elliott to take the script with him to rehab and study the lines. I was naïve. I had no idea how much work it would take for Elliott to go through detox, focus on himself, and work through the underlying issues that made him want to take drugs in the first place.

I got to the high school in the morning after first period. I parked my car at the visitor parking area. It was raining. I was still in a daze from finding out my son was a heroin addict and then dropping him off at his first rehabilitation institutional facility. That little voice in the back of my mind kept saying, "This isn't real. This isn't happening … Oh my God, I'm going to be sick …"

I walked up the front steps to the school, hoping I wouldn't see anyone I knew and have to explain why I was there. *Just look down at the wet concrete walkway,* I thought. *Don't make eye contact. Give off that leave-me-the-hell-alone vibe, and you'll be fine.*

I made it to the front doors. It took everything I had to grab the door handle and pull. The door felt like it weighed two hundred pounds. Everything was in slow motion. I made it to the front office and signed in. The school had an open design, and I had to walk back outside and around the building to get to the drama department. I opened the exterior door with my heart in my throat. *Don't cry. Don't cry. Composure.*

The students were sitting in a corner of the room practicing their lines for the upcoming production. They looked up at me as the door opened. I asked for Greta, and one of the students pointed to the back of the room where a door led to the backstage. I thanked the student and walked toward the door, trying not to listen to the murmurs of the students as I passed them. Did they know? How could they know if I, Elliott's mother, didn't?

Greta was sitting with another student talking as I approached her. They were behind the curtains of the little theater—the same theater where Elliott worked his magic during a production or an improv match. Who knew the back of the curtains were black? The student Greta was talking to recognized me. She didn't smile to greet me. Maybe it was the look on my face; she knew I had bad news. She just looked at me really quick, stood up, and walked out. *Did she know?*

Greta welcomed me to sit down. She was so comforting. I felt like I was a student and wanted to throw my arms around her and cry.

Instead, I sat down and told her everything. She put her arm around my shoulders and let me weep as I tried to tell her my story of why Elliot, her star actor, would not be coming to drama practice for the month. She had no idea the severity of the problem. Kids get high from smoking weed or sniffing glue, but smoking heroin was a whole other ordeal. Was she thinking of sweaty, skinny, dirty men?

She couldn't understand my pain, and I then realized that I had just given her a problem that she would have to solve—getting a replacement for the lead role and have him ready to perform in a month and a half. I thanked her for her kindness, and with my head hung low, I walked out and back through the classroom without looking at the students before quickly heading back to my car. *Get me the hell out of here—and now,* was all I thought.

Being the parent of a drug addict is horrendous. Other parents judge you. I know because I did. What role did you play with why your child needed to get high? Why would your child want to use drugs? What was he trying to escape? What were you doing to make his life that miserable? What kind of mother are you? Were you using drugs?

Thirty-two

August 2013 - Nick

I KNEW I NEEDED TO GET BACK TO DATING AFTER BREAKING THINGS OFF WITH David. Those feelings of loneliness and the deep yearning you get when you've lost someone close hit me like a ton of bricks. The lack of physical touch, whether it's holding someone's hand or sitting close to someone on the couch, emphasized the loss. *Great, I'm alone again. How long will this spurt last?* All those feelings pulled me closer to making that call to David or driving over to his house. So, I took out an insurance policy, so to speak. I got online … Yep, back to online dating for me. I chose a dating site for people fifty and older. I did not want to get matched with Blake or some younger man looking for a sugar mama who was going to take care of him. No more taking care of a man. I wanted someone who was financially stable, maybe owned a home, and was happy with his job and life in general. I wanted the opposite of what I had with Blake but also someone who had the balls to see reality and do what needed to be done—someone who didn't stick his head in deep sand so he couldn't see a dose of truth no matter how difficult the truth was.

I created my profile, threw in a few recent photos, and started looking at the available victims. I had loads of spare time—the time I had been spending with David—so I was online looking for hours. Any man I found within fifty miles with an attractive face I clicked on or sent a stupid message like "hey" or "hi there" … Let's get something going. Let's find someone to fill the excruciating blank-hole-like feeling I was sinking into.

I started getting responses from guys hundreds of miles away. Are you kidding me? I went out with a few interesting faces who were closer to my area. Nothing—no sparks. Then I saw a profile with one photo that wasn't really clear and kind of dark. There wasn't a whole lot of information with it either. I sent a message: "You need to put more photos and information in your profile."

Within a few hours, I got a response. "Why would I do that?"

"To get more interest, duh," was my response.

"Well, I've got you messaging me now, don't I?" was what came back.

What kind of arrogant comment was that? Then, wouldn't you know it, the .com found us to be a match. I practically fell out of my chair. How stupid! This dating site made any two people a match if they lived within thirty miles of each other.

I sent this man Nick Peterson, who was bantering with me, a message: "Hey, look at that. We are a match."

The response came back suggesting we go out for coffee. God, that was the last thing I wanted to do. Sitting across a small table at a crowded coffee shop making stupid small talk while I was nervously sweating and trying to sound smart didn't appeal to me. I've been in coffee shops and overheard those conversations. No thank you! I suggested we do something like play pool or take a hike—something that would take away my nervous energy and keep our eyes from having to be locked onto each other as we noticed little flaws in the way we dressed or twitched our mouths while talking.

I suggested we meet at a park near my neighborhood. He didn't like that idea, as his ex-wife lived within blocks of me, and he didn't want to take the chance of bumping into her. *OK*, I thought. *Maybe there's still some kind of feelings there for an ex-wife, but it could be revulsion instead of love—who knows. And hey, at least it was an ex-wife he was concerned with, not some soon-to-be ex-wife or just plain-old wife!* So, we agreed on a park near his residence the following Tuesday.

Of course, I hadn't been over to that side of the city in a long while and wasn't sure where the park was located. I must not have known how to use GPS on my phone yet because I found myself a bit lost at the time I was supposed to be at this park. I pulled over and texted him and then turned around and headed back in the direction where the park was supposed to be. Yes, I had passed it. I finally got to the park and found a parking spot, which wasn't easy. I walked to the park and got on the walking path that went around a large lake located in the middle. I had no idea what this guy really looked like because the photo in his profile was too blurry and dark to make out his features. I didn't know how tall he was or what he was wearing. I was relying on him to recognize me from the various photos I had posted on my dating profile. All I knew was he was probably pissed at how late I was (forty-five minutes), and he was walking one direction while I was walking the other direction on this walking path, so eventually we would pass each other.

I was wearing khaki shorts and a white tank top and felt like I looked good, especially after I turned a few heads from strangers who weren't Nick. Nothing like a little turn of the head to boost one's confidence just before meeting a new dating prospect. Then, as I was walking along the path, I passed a gentleman who said my name in a questioning way. I stopped and turned, and there he was—a man who was nothing like the type I would typically choose. This guy wasn't tall and overpowering like I usually was attracted to; he was probably five ten with a full head of hair (nice) and dressed in khakis and a white polo shirt. How cute—our outfits matched. Conservative Republican oozed out of his pores, and I immediately thought, *Nope, he's not going to like me.* However, before writing him off, I felt something inside telling me to give him a chance. *He may be nice. He may be worthy of you.*

I decided to hold nothing back. Instead of trying to impress this man, I was going to just be my energetic, strange, passionate, goofy self, and if he didn't like it, then he could just move along. I asked him what he did for a living, and he told me he was an attorney. Defense or plaintiff was my next question. *Plaintiff… Ugh, he's on the dark side,* I thought. *He's on the opposite side of the insurance defense team.* I was surprised I hadn't met him before while working some of my insurance claims.

I asked him what his most interesting case had been. He proceeded to share a case he'd recently lost, and when I say lost, I mean lost *big.* He represented a woman whose leg was run over by a bus. The city had offered $1 million, but he felt it was worth several million more, so he took the case to trial. One thing after another happened … yada, yada, yada … and the jury awarded the insurance company a defense verdict … He and his client got a big fat *zero.* Now being on the other side of the fence handling insurance defense claims I found this story funny and giggled. Normally, if I were trying to impress a date, I would have showed sympathy, but I wasn't about to put on a charade.

He was a bit shocked at my giggles, and I noticed him stop and pause, jerking his head back slightly as if he needed to take a better look at me, maybe in disbelief that I found such a gut-wrenching story humorous. But he had to know how I would feel being from the other side. He then asked me about my most memorable claim. We ended up talking and laughing as we made it back to where we started our walk together. The time went by so fast, and I wasn't done. Obviously, he wasn't either, as he asked if I wanted to go across the street for a beer. This was nice—this open talking with a man I'd never met before. There was no deep look and comment that he was going to marry me someday like my last first date.

We crossed the street and sat at the bar. He told me he was a yell leader in high school. "Yell leader?" I questioned. "You mean cheerleader, right?" Nope, the guys were referred to as yell leaders. Whatever. I was a cheerleader in high school and for three years in college at the University of Denver. I won. I even showed him a cheer my college squad did for our rivals where we ended with a sequence of arm movements that was basically flipping the other team off. We were the heathens, and the other team was the self-righteous, holier-than-though team. It was expected of us! Nick laughed.

After a few hours, I realized I needed to get home to my two younger kids who were both old enough to take care of themselves, Melissa in high school and Elliott working full time but college-aged. He walked me to my car, and I drove him to his—or what he said was his—car. At first, I didn't believe him. It was a beautiful maroon Jaguar. *Yeah right. He is just saying this is his car, so I can be impressed. He will probably walk toward the Jag, and then as soon as I drive off, he will proceed down the street to his Chevy Malibu or Volkswagen.*

I was in the driver's seat, and he looked over at me to say goodbye. He leaned in, and for some strange reason, I followed. He kissed me, so I kissed him back. He had a unique mouth—did I already tell you that? Well, it was one of the first things I noticed about him after his full, thick head of hair, which is rare in an older man—not that there's anything wrong with bald. Bald is beautiful, but what can I say? I prefer hair.

I wasn't expecting to see him for a while, as he told me that the following week, he would be in Aspen at his cabin ... with his kids. Sure ... I thought it was probably with another woman, but who cared? I had just met the guy. So, I drove home, and that night and every night afterward until he eventually moved in three years later, he sent me a text saying, "Good night, Ms. Byers," until it became Mrs. Peterson five years later. But I guess he needed to see me one more time before he left for the cabin because he asked if he could take me to dinner that Friday night. I obliged, and he picked me up right on time with a dozen roses ... in his maroon Jaguar.

I tell you about Nick because this man didn't just change my life. He changed my son's life. Unlike Elliott's father, this man was happy with his life, was happy with his work, had a positive outlook, and was a pure gentleman—the open-your-door-type gentleman, the old-fashioned, don't-eat-until-everyone-is-served gentleman. He was not tall, dark, dashing, and daring like the type I usually fell for. He was sweet, kind, and polite. It wasn't long before I realized he had all the good qualities of my dad. Maybe it's true about the saying how a girl's first love is her dad ... that, or I had daddy issues.

Nick's influences didn't have a big impact on Elliott until they were both living under the same roof.

Thirty-three

November/December 2012 - Rehab One

When Elliott was in the first rehabilitation center, we came every weekend for parent visitation and group sessions. The leader had activities planned for each visit. Blake and I would drive down together to save on gas. At the first visit, we were led to a large room where it looked like lunch was served, as there were lunch tables leaning up against a wall, and chairs were set up in a circle. The kids came out, and my eyes searched for my Elliott. Once I spotted him, that's all there was—tunnel vision to Elliott.

Clean Elliott had a different look to him. His eyes seemed clearer; his features were sharper; he was back in the real world. He saw me and smiled. I ran to him and wrapped my arms around him. He hugged me back. After a good, long, hard hug where I was trying to tell him with my arm strength how much I loved him, I stepped back and allowed Blake to do the same. My tunnel vision opened, and I started seeing the other kids in Elliott's group. All of them looked like juvenile delinquents; most of them were. The majority of the kids were African American, Mexican, or Native American. There were a few Caucasians, but like Elliott, they stuck out like a sore thumb. Elliott was the rich white kid, although we were nowhere near rich … but to these kids, we were. I continued hearing my voice in the back of my mind: "How did this happen? This is unreal. This isn't happening. Oh my God."

For some kids, this was their second or third time in rehab, and their parents didn't come to the visitations and group sessions anymore. Some of the kids were there by a court order … juvenile delinquents. Elliott was instantly good friends with all of them. He started talking like them and acting like them. He would walk with that jive-turkey strut sometimes, and I just thought, *Is this place going to help him or make him worse?* I looked at each kid in the group and wanted to know their stories. Why were they here? What drove them to get to this place in their lives? What was their DOC (Drug Of Choice)? What were their families like? Were their parents divorced too? What were their siblings like? I wanted to take them all and fix them.

Some of the kids had one parent there, but Elliott was the only one with both his mom and dad there to help. We all engaged in introductions and then started having group therapy. It became obvious that all of these kids had been working hard to help themselves. Several of the mothers had doubt on their faces as their son or daughter would talk about getting better and getting out to start fresh and be a productive member of society. Those mothers had heard it all before, and there they were, listening to it again for the umpteenth time. This was my first time hearing my son talk about how hard he was working there in the rehab center and how hard he was going to continue working so I would be proud of him. I was already proud of him, and if he continued staying clean, I would continue staying proud.

Thirty-four

Autumn 2013 - Stalker

A COUPLE OF WEEKS AFTER I STARTED DATING NICK, DAVID STARTED CALLING. He needed me to come over and pick up some of my things that were still at his house. I agreed to come over, and as I drove down the long street to his house, a rush of feelings went through me. What were these feelings? Was I feeling melancholy? Sadness? Nervousness? What was I going to feel when I saw David's face?

I parked my car in his gravel driveway and got out of the car. He was waiting for me and was walking over from his front door. I got out of my car and watched him as he approached. I felt sorry for him. I wasn't sad. I didn't feel a loss when I saw him. Instead, I felt sorry that he wasn't going to get what he wanted from me. I knew he wanted to get back together. I could tell how he walked up to me and put his arms around me. He gave a big sigh, pulled me close, and then kissed the top of my head as if I had been gone but was now back to stay.

I pulled away from him and looked up into his watery eyes. He was about to cry. *Oh God, no. I must put a stop to this immediately.* "I've met someone. He's really nice." That's all I said.

"Oh, I see," he said. It was so clumsy and awkward. "I miss you. I love you so much."

"Thank you. I know it's new and all, but I don't want to hurt this guy. I think he likes me." I sounded like a little schoolgirl and felt stupid. I wanted to get my stuff and get the hell out of there. But he was pleading with me to stay and talk. He wanted to assure me that everything was getting better. Dustin was clean now and getting a job. My eyes just rolled inside my head. It took everything I had not to shake my head back and forth and tell him that I didn't believe him. I just took my things, said thank you, and got back into my car.

He bent down; his face was right outside my window. He started tapping on it with his finger and asking that I roll it down. I didn't. I backed up and drove away like the drama queen that I was. I was wearing that crown loud and proud.

I had something good—something real. I wasn't going to jeopardize it for David, the man who couldn't face reality and do what needed to be done.

Soon, David was texting and calling me every day. I blocked him. Then I noticed his red Ford truck driving by my office and my house. I was at my office one morning, and he called. He was crying. I felt sorry for him. He calmed down quickly and told me that Adam was wondering where Grandma was ... It was his weapon of the day: Adam. Sweet, little Adam, the boy who called me Grandma ... whom I adored. I believed him. I missed that boy, and I'm sure he missed me too. But David's little game wasn't going to work on me. No Adam, or Adam's mom, whom I both adored, were going to make me get back together with David. I told him I had to go; I couldn't talk to him at work. I told him to get help, and if I heard from him again, I would file a restraining order against him and hung up. I immediately called human resources and reported the call and my concerns. I gave them his cell number so they could prevent him from calling into my office.

A month or so later, Melissa and I were in TJ Maxx, my favorite shopping experience. There's nothing like finding a $900 bag for $80 or a $300 pair of pants for $25. It was a rush. One of our favorite mother/daughter dates would be to go to TJ Maxx, fill a cart with deals, and then go to the family dressing room and try everything on. After we tried things on, we would set aside the clothes that fit and looked good to one end of the room with a pile for the definite purchases and maybes. After everything was tried on and put in its particular pile, we would decide if we were going to buy it. Most of the time we would walk out of the store with only purchasing a few items, sometimes nothing. It just depended on what we found and our moods ... and budget.

One of those times I was looking through a clearance rack, and there David was walking up to me with a smug smile on his face. "Hey, you. How are you doing? I thought I might find you in here. Every time I drive by, I look for your car."

Oh, that's just great to know. Next time I'll need to drive a different car. Those were my thoughts. "Hello," was all I said.

David then started a conversation as if I cared. He brought me up to date with the latest news concerning all of his kids, and of course, they were all doing great. He would look at my ring finger on my left hand and comment about how I wasn't engaged yet ... as if that meant I was still available and there was still hope for him.

I kept shopping, sometimes turning my back to him and walking away. He followed me and continued talking as if I wanted him to and we were there together. Sometimes Melissa would spot us and come over to my rescue. "Hey, Mom. Want to go try on some of these clothes?"

David said hi to Melissa, who gave him a quick hello and came between us, putting her arm around me as if to say to David, "She's *mine*."

He got the hint, said goodbye, and walked out of the store, nothing in hand. His sole purpose of going into the store was not to buy a shirt or socks. It was because he saw my car parked in the parking lot, and he wanted to come talk to me.

There were many encounters like that. One time when he was bringing me up to date on Dustin and how well he was doing, I asked him, "Is he still constipated?"

Oh, Dustin had a job and was going to school, and he was clean. "Yes, but he's still dealing with that constipation problem," he would reply with an embarrassed giggle and his hand over his mouth.

I looked straight into his brown eyes and told him, "Then he's still using."

David was stunned. He couldn't fool me. He just stood there frozen with his mouth open and no words coming out.

I told him, "He's constipated from the heroin. It's called opioid constipation." Inside, I was screaming: *You idiot! Open your eyes!* But I didn't say it out loud. I just looked at him. He must have heard my internal screaming because he succumbed to my laser looks and admitted that I was probably right. I walked away in disgust.

Ten minutes later, he snuck up on me in the housewares section—the nerve of that man. I was looking at frying pans when he pleaded, "Please don't tell anyone." I just looked at him in disbelief, and this time outwardly shook my head. He didn't want to see it, he didn't want to admit to it, and he didn't want anyone to know about it. He was embarrassed and ashamed, as if he had something to do with it. He would rather hide the truth, as it may be a reflection of himself. Nothing was further than the truth, but he didn't want to open his mind and learn more about it—about the addiction or the drug itself. He didn't want to learn that there were millions of parents just like himself. I was one of them, a woman whose child was a heroin addict, and it was OK. There was something you could do about it. You didn't have to hide it. You could get help like I did.

Thirty-five

December 2012 - Christmas
after First Rehab

BRANDON CAME HOME FROM TEXAS FOR CHRISTMAS. WE PICKED HIM UP AT the airport and then drove down to the facility from there. Elliott had convinced his counselor and the staff that he was good and ready to come home and start a new life. He convinced all of us that he was going to stay clean for the rest of his life. He worked so hard to get through the detox process and do all of the rehab assignments for the last three weeks. He wasn't going to do that over again. The facility agreed to let Elliott go early so he could be home for Christmas.

It was a joyous occasion. Elliott was coming home, and he was going to stay clean! It was a new day—a fresh start. Everything was going to be OK.

That joyous feeling didn't last long. Elliott was home a few days before Christmas, and on the day after Christmas, he was passed out on the couch high on heroin. Christmas day was nice. The kids and I exchanged one gift each on Christmas Eve and watched Christmas movies before going to bed. We got up that morning. Melissa was thirteen years old and woke up first and then woke up her brothers to start the festivities of unwrapping gifts and emptying stockings. Later, I had David and his kids over for Christmas dinner, which was awkward, but we lived through it. Dustin slept during the meal, which I later found out was due to his heroin high. He sat across the table from me, and I looked over at him once and noticed his chin resting on his chest. He wasn't talking or eating, just sitting there sleeping. David commented that he must have been up late last night playing video games. How funny … how cute … Dustin was high as a kite from heroin on Christmas day.

The next day was the day Christmas came down. After having my house cluttered with Santas and snowmen splashed everywhere for the past month I was done and wanted a cleaner, simpler feeling. The kids were sleeping in, and

I started early. Santa figurines of all sorts and shapes and sizes, snowmen, the nativity scene, candles, and holiday pillows were put into plastic bins and back onto the storage shelves in the shed and hall. I was taking decorations off the tree when Elliott came out from his room and grabbed some breakfast.

His friend from high school drama, Mary Stalwart, knocked on the door. Elliott ran to the door and let her in. The two of them sat at the dining room table. Elliott was super happy and talkative, telling Mary all about his experience at rehab. Something wasn't right. Elliott wasn't the same as when I picked him up from rehab, but I couldn't put my finger on it. What was different?

Brandon soon woke up and knew right away. Elliott was high. Mary Stalwart left after a brief visit, and Brandon sat down at the table where Elliott had basically passed out. His head was down on his arm, and he was asleep. Brandon reached over the table and put his hand on Elliott's arm. Brandon started shaking Elliott's arm and saying his name to wake him up. Groggy Elliott lifted his head and looked at Brandon.

It was too much for Brandon. He started talking to Elliott in a stern but shaking voice. "What are you doing, Elliott? Look at yourself. I know you're high. Why would you do this? Is this really what you want to do with your life?"

I was standing on my step stool taking shiny red glass balls off my Christmas tree and putting them back into their cardboard containers with a cold, heavy ball in my gut as I watched my oldest son crying. Brandon was pleading through his tears as he tried to get through to his younger brother. Elliott was deep in a heroin high. My heart was breaking. Brandon, although eight years older, loved his little brother, and it was killing him to see Elliott fall back to a level he had just gotten out of. For a mother to watch her oldest son cry and plead with his younger brother to stop something that may kill him was unbearable.

I failed. I shouldn't have let Elliott come home early. He needed more time. This overpowering selfish feeling came over me. How could I have been so stupid? This was heroin! This wasn't some wamsy-pamsy drug. This drug was killing people left and right. What was I thinking that Elliott could stop using heroin after a mere detox and three weeks of rehab? Shit. It was time for plan B.

Thirty-six

December 2012 to February 2013 -
Baby Girl and Cheek Blockers

A FEW NIGHTS AFTER THE CHRISTMAS DECORATIONS WERE TAKEN DOWN, Melissa came to me with a secret. It was a secret she was afraid to tell me. She had tears running down her beautiful white cheeks as she was weeping. "It's my fault, Mom! I bought him the lighter. He promised me he wouldn't use it for heroin, but he did, Mom. I shouldn't have taken him to the store and bought the lighter."

I wrapped my arms around my weeping daughter and told her, "No, no, no. It's his choice. You had nothing to do with his choice, Melissa. Only *he* can choose to use." My sweet baby girl was blaming herself for Elliott's faltering back to heroin use.

Plan B was to see a children's addiction specialist. We were scheduled to see Dr. Andrew Chew at Children's Hospital Colorado. I still had hope. *Do what the doctor says. Follow the rules. We can beat this. I'll do anything.*

You know how when you're sick and have called the doctor and scheduled an appointment, for some reason you start feeling better? That's how I felt. I had someone to help me—someone who I could rely on to point me in the right direction.

We met with Dr. Chew together, Blake, me, and Elliott. He suggested having Elliott take blockers, which were prescription pills that blocked the effects of heroin. Elliott agreed to do it. Great. Elliott was willing to help himself! Several weeks went by, with an appointment with Dr. Chew each week. Elliott was taking the blockers; everything was going great—or so I thought. It was like watching a stupid movie where you can tell what is about to happen, and it's no surprise when it does—very predictable.

Blake stopped coming to the appointments because work was too busy and much more important. Elliott and I went to Children's Hospital Colorado and walked the hallways to Dr. Chew's office. Elliott went in first. I sat in the waiting room skimming through magazines and looking at the tropical fish in the aquarium. Elliott came out and told me it was my turn.

"All righty. Thanks, Elliott," I said as I stood up, put the magazine down, and made my way to Dr. Chew's office. I sat down and looked up at Dr. Chew who was sitting at his desk facing me with his elbows down and hands clasped together.

"Well, Elliott has been cheeking the blockers," he announced.

Cheeking? I wondered. *What the hell does that mean?*

"Elliott told me that he doesn't want to stop using right now. He says he'll stop when he's ready." There was a long pause … He was letting that bit of news sink into my blurry brain, thoughts swirling around so fast I was getting lightheaded. "In the state of Colorado, his age allows him to choose his medical treatment. I know of a facility in Wyoming you need to have him taken to."

Taken to? What the hell do you mean by that? Of course, I was only thinking those words. I was stunned in my seat, unable to speak as I was hearing all of this.

"The facility is called Mountain West Behavioral. Call them to see if they have an opening. They usually have a waiting list." He then handed me a business card for Mountain West Behavioral as he stood up to see me out of his office.

And the wind was knocked out of me again. I walked out of his office and into the lobby where Elliott was waiting. He stood up and looked me in the eye. He held his head high with no remorse. He knew what he wanted and knew I had just been given the news. Again, he had been lying to me about taking his blockers, now he was taking his life in his own hands, and he felt good about it. He had no idea what Dr. Chew had recommended, and I wasn't going to tell him. *Let him think he has everything under control, I don't care. I'll do what the doctor says.*

We walked out of the hospital and to the car. I put my hand on Elliott's back and gave him a love-rub, trying to let him know through my hands that I loved him no matter what. Inside my head and heart, I was thinking, *I'm not stopping, my sweet boy … You think you are getting what you want but I've got something else in mind.* My mother-muscles were bulging … never give up, never surrender.

Elliot and I drove home from Children's Hospital Colorado and didn't talk much. My mind was racing as to what I needed to do next. As soon as I could, I had to contact Blake to tell him what happened at the doctor's meeting. It would have been nice if he could have made this a priority, but I wasn't surprised. Blake and his needs were always his first priority. The next call would be to Mountain West Behavioral to see if there was an opening or to get in line to have Elliott accepted into their program.

We got home after the drive of silence with Elliott thinking he was going to continue using heroin until he was ready to quit and my thoughts racing about getting him into an out-of-state rehabilitation center recommended by the pediatric addiction doctor. I couldn't let Elliott know my secret plan, or he might run.

The first rehabilitation center recommended that we change Elliott's bedroom so he wouldn't come back to the same things that may trigger a craving. My small 1,600-square-foot home had three bedrooms, so we did a complete rearrangement of rooms. Elliott's room was too small to change the furniture, so we just moved stuff. Melissa refused to move into Elliott's room where he used heroin. I understood that. What thirteen-year-old girl would want to sleep in the same bed where her older brother would smoke heroin and blow chunks in his wastebasket? I had no choice. I moved my stuff into Elliott's small room, Melissa's stuff moved into my bedroom, and Elliott's stuff moved into Melissa's bedroom. What a mother won't do for her children. I didn't care how uncomfortable I was. I'd do anything to help my son and keep my daughter from screaming.

We got home and were getting out of the car when Elliott told me he wanted to go see Jeffrey. I knew where he was going and what he was planning on doing, but I let him go. I needed the time for the phone calls I didn't want him to overhear. As soon as he left the house, I called Blake. He was disappointed with Elliott and on board with Dr. Chew's recommendation. One call down. One call to go.

I called Mountain West Behavioral. I introduced myself and told the lady on the other end of the line that they were recommended to me by Dr. Chew with Children's Hospital Colorado. I could hear the trepidation in my voice as if I were trying to explain this everyday occurrence that every American family experiences at least once if not twice a year. The lady on the other end took my information and said someone would be getting back to me.

The next day they called me back. There was a waiting list. *So be it*, I thought. *Put his name on the list.* And the waiting game began.

Thirty-seven

February 2013 - Laundry—Throwing Up

A FEW DAYS LATER I WAS DOING A LOAD OF LAUNDRY AND NOTICED ELLIOTT'S door was closed. I opened his door, knocking first, of course, to prevent my eyes from seeing anything private yet healthy. Elliott was sitting up in his bed with the plastic wastebasket in his lap as he was throwing up. He had just smoked heroin. It's one of the side effects; it makes you throw up immediately afterward. Elliott looked up at me as he was leaning over the wastebasket, mouth wide open, and puke spewing out. He held up one finger as if to communicate with me because his mouth and digestive system were busy at the time. His one finger was telling me, "Hold on one minute. I'm busy yacking." I couldn't watch. I looked down and closed the door, telling Elliott that I was doing a load of darks and to bring me his dark clothes if he wanted them washed.

Oh my God. How much more can I take? Let there be an opening at Mountain West Behavioral soon ... Let there be an opening soon ... Let there be an opening soon ... Breathe.

Elliott had stopped staying at his dad's apartment. Maybe self-absorbed individuals don't mix well with drug addicts, who knows. All I knew was Elliott was back at school, if that's what you wanted to call it, and hanging out with the same friend Jeffrey. Watching the heroin high and trying to ignore it was wearing thin on my nerves. I wasn't sleeping well in Elliott's small room, and the fear of how this may be affecting Melissa was heavy on my mind.

One night when Elliott was slouching on the couch watching television, I broke. The kitchen had dirty dishes in the sink and a frying pan still sitting on the stove with the remnants of scrambled eggs still stuck to the bottom. Elliott's room had clothes thrown all over the floor and the puke basket was still sitting on his bed ready to be used again. I came home from work and walked through the kitchen and past Elliott's room.

As I stepped into the family room, Elliott looked up at me. There was no, "Hey, Mom. How was work?" Just a glassy-eyed stare.

"You're high again, aren't you?" I asked him.

He just looked at me and nodded his head in a yes response. That nod felt like he was saying, "Oh, yes I am high as a kite from heroin, and whatcha gonna to do about it?"

Part of me thought, *Well, at least he's being honest*, but another part was pissed.

Just then, Melissa came in with her friend Colleen. Melissa and Colleen went to the same gymnastics facility. Both had great potential but lacked the kind of motivation necessary to be high-level gymnasts. Colleen had recently moved with her mother and siblings to California but was back in Colorado visiting her dad and friends, Melissa included. I couldn't bear to have them seeing Elliott on a heroin high. They went in Melissa's room, my old room with the attached private bathroom … how I missed that room.

That was when I snapped. I told Elliott I couldn't have him doing heroin in my house. I felt like I had to protect Melissa somehow. *Not in my house.*

Elliott looked at me, his eyes glossy and red. "I'll go to a friend's house or dad's." Elliott was simply fine with the idea of leaving. Maybe he understood. "I need money for a bus," Elliott said as he looked at me.

I loved that kid so much, but I also loved Melissa and couldn't stand having Elliott getting his heroin high on around her. I ran to my purse, hoping to have something and found some coins. I took those coins and went back to Elliott. I threw three quarters at him. "Here. Go take the bus. This is all I've got. Just get out of the house. I can't have you here like that."

And he left. My heart broke … again. I couldn't expose Melissa to his heroin high. I just couldn't.

He went to his dad's place, and that's where he stayed until we got the call a few weeks later. Mountain West Behavioral had an opening.

Thirty-eight

April 2013 – Kidnapped and Delivered to 2nd Rehab

MOUNTAIN WEST BEHAVIORAL COULD TAKE ELLIOTT IN THREE DAYS. THEY gave us the name and contact information of a service they use to "pick up" kids and deliver them to their facility. We called them and told them the day they needed to come and get Elliott. Blake gave them his address. Elliott stayed with him and used his heroin without judgment after I told him to get out of my house if he was going to get his heroin high around Melissa. Blake agreed to do everything he could to make sure Elliott was at his place when they showed up.

April 2, 2013, at two o'clock in the morning was the last time Elliott smoked heroin. Two hours later, at around four thirty that morning, I drove up to Blake's apartment just as the "pickup and delivery" company arrived. Two husky individuals, a male and female, opened the doors and got out of what appeared to be a retired unmarked police car. I walked up to them, extending a hand to shake and asked if they were there to pick up Elliott. They were both in uniform, and the gentleman took my hand in his and squeezed.

Good morning. I'm Karen, the mother of the heroin-addicted boy you are kidnapping this morning and taking to a rehabilitation facility. How are you? This sick feeling came over me. I couldn't believe this was actually happening. I was having my son forcefully taken out of the state and delivered to another state with different laws that didn't give teenagers a choice on how to be medically treated. I was having Elliott put into a recovery center in hopes that their treatment would work.

I walked the silverback-gorilla-sized humans to Blake's apartment entrance where Blake was up waiting. We led them quietly up the stairs to the bedroom where Elliott was sleeping. We slowly opened the door, and the two uniformed individuals asked for Blake and I to step away in case Elliott decided to bolt. The stories they could probably tell. We backed up into the hall and watched the scene play out in front of us.

The woman was the size of three of me and approached the top of the bed. She leaned over Elliott's head, gently trying to wake him. The uniformed mammoth of a man went to the side and end of the bed, bracing himself as if ready to tackle Elliott if he put up a fight. Elliott was obviously groggy from his heroin-induced sleep and mumbled to the two strangers, asking what was going on. My heart broke as I heard the fear in his voice. The gigantic woman told him they were there to take him to a place that was going to help him.

Then it was quiet. Elliott pulled on the jeans that were left on the floor and threw on a shirt. It felt like Elliott was accepting his fate; there would be no fight. The kidnappers asked Elliott to put his hands behind his back, and they gently put a zip tie around his wrists. With my new huge, uniformed friends taking an arm on each side, he was led down the stairs and out of Blake's apartment. I followed them as they walked down the sidewalk toward the car. The back-passenger door was opened, and they gently put Elliott in the back, pushing his head down so he wouldn't bump it as he entered the vehicle. My heart was pounding out of my chest. I could feel it in my stomach … All I could hear was my heart beating.

Elliott sat quietly in the middle of the back seat. Turned out, the vehicle being used to deliver Elliott really was a retired unmarked police car. This was good because the back-seat area had no interior handles for Elliott to open and run. They asked Blake and I if we wanted to say something to Elliott before they left. I approached the front seat of the car and leaned in, looking at Elliott in the back through a screened middle section that separated the front from the back. Elliott just looked at me with hatred in his dark eyes.

"I love you, Elliott. I love you." That's all I could say. The pleaser in me wanted to say I was sorry, but I wouldn't let it … *I'm not sorry. I'm doing this to help you.* I couldn't say anything but "I love you" … that was the strongest feeling I could give him.

Elliott did not respond. He just stared at me. I backed up to allow Blake his chance to say his farewells and stepped up onto the sidewalk. Then they were gone. I watched as the unmarked delivery car drove off, hoping maybe Elliott would turn his head back and see me watching them go with tears welling up in my eyes. Then he would know how painful this was for me—how the pain radiated through me to the bone. I was cold and shaking, not because of the temperature outside but because of the intense emotions running through my veins. Blake gave me a hug, and we agreed to stay in touch and drive down every weekend together to visit. I then got into my car. I put both hands on the steering wheel, dropped my head, closed my eyes, and breathed just to steady myself before turning the key. That was when I realized I wasn't just a mother. I was one strong motherfucker. And then I started driving back home.

I got off the 105 exit to Salsbury Street and stopped to check traffic before making my right-hand turn. Just as I finished the turn onto Salsbury and was heading home to where Melissa was still sleeping in her bed, an owl flew across the street right in front of my windshield. It startled me, but I took it as a sign—a sign that I did the right thing. My heart lifted, and for the first time in several months, I felt hope. *Cling to this feeling*, I told myself. *Stretch it out and carry it close … The work is only beginning.*

Thirty-nine

April 2013 - Mountain West Behavioral

THE FOLLOWING DAY, MOUNTAIN WEST BEHAVIORAL FACILITY CALLED TO confirm that Elliott made it and was checked in. They crossed the state line and made it. There was a list of items that Elliott needed while he was there, which they emailed over to both Blake and me. Elliott was going through his second detox and unable to talk on the phone, but they assured us he was fine and would be able to talk in a couple of days … after the cold sweat and shivering of detox wore off. Blake and I agreed to what each of us would purchase on the list and bring with us during our first visit in about a week.

I was able to speak with Elliott after a few days, and he begged to come home. "I don't need to be here, Mom. I can stop on my own, Mom, I promise. I'll stop. Just get me out of here."

How I wanted to believe him, but how I knew that three weeks at the last rehabilitation center wasn't long enough, and I wasn't going to fall for that assurance again. Nope. Elliott was in it for the long haul this time: four weeks … I only hoped that would be long enough.

Flashbacks of David telling me that Dustin was treating himself came flooding back. "He's treating himself. He knows what he needs to do. He doesn't need a doctor. Why should I pay a doctor who just gives him a prescription?" I stayed strong as steel and would not allow Elliott's words to pull so hard on my heart that I gave in. They pulled, all right, but not hard enough. I wouldn't let them. *Be strong. Be tough. Elliott needs you to be strong for him.* The first rehab didn't work, and I allowed him to get out early—not this time. This time Elliott was going to stay the entire time and get everything he could out of this experience. There are no short cuts with heroin; it's too strong. *Heroin's pull on Elliott is stronger than Elliott's pull on my heart strings right now. I must be stronger than the heroin addiction pull … for Elliott, my sweet boy.*

The drive to Wyoming was four hours or so, depending on traffic. Blake and I took turns driving. I drove the first weekend and played Eric Church's *Chief* album most of the way down. We drove in and parked. This place was different than the first. Mountain West Behavioral had group session first for the parents of new students. They served coffee, juice, and pastries. We all took turns sharing our experiences and why we were there. Not everyone was there for drug-addiction issues. Some families were there due to psychological issues, suicide attempts, and minor criminal problems. This facility focused more on the behavioral roots of problems. What was the cause of the attempted suicide, outburst at authorities, assaults on family members, use of cocaine, meth, heroin, or whatever else? What was the underlying reasons? They didn't just put a bandage on the problem. Put the client through detox, give him or her some group therapy sessions, and voilà, the person is cured! No, this place put the client through detox and then started a deep dig into the psyche. Barry was Elliott's counselor. Barry was a recovered addict now giving back.

After our group session with the other parents, we were able to meet up with Elliott, who continued to tell us that he didn't need to be there and asked us to please let him come home with us. We held strong and assured Elliott that he was not coming home until he finished the program this time. My heart broke as I told him no, but I knew this was something I had to do.

Forty

Monster Talk

I HAD TO LOOK AT ELLIOTT LIKE HE WAS POSSESSED BY A MONSTER; THE MONSTER for him was heroin. I remember when I was a brace-and-pimple-faced teenager watching a movie where aliens came down to Earth in large, furry brown pods. When a human got near the pod, it would slowly crack open with green ooze strings stretching between the edges of the cracks. The alien would then quickly absorb itself into the human body, completely taking over. The human still looked the same, but something was off. It's really no different with addiction. Elliott still looked the same, like my handsome athletic boy bringing back memories of playing Legos and taking him trick-or-treating when he was a sweet little toddler. But he wasn't my boy anymore. He was a heroin monster on the outside, and my beautiful son was getting smaller and smaller as he was transcending deep inside his human body, letting the heroin take over.

I had to treat the monster the way it deserved to be treated … ruthlessly. I had to set my boundaries with specific rules in my house—rules that would support his recovery and punish his heroin use, the monster. It only costs ten dollars for a small bag of heroin. "Mom, can I borrow ten bucks for lunch?" Shoot, you can't get a decent lunch at Subway for less than ten dollars. Instead of giving the money to the little monster, I told him to make his own lunch and made sure I had food in the fridge. Ham and cheese, his favorite, were always in abundant supply.

If you are nice to the monster, it stays longer. If you give the monster what it wants (money), it stays longer. If you make the monster comfortable, it never wants to leave, and it won't. I was afraid that the monster would stay and grow while my son shrunk—shrunk until he no longer existed.

I'll never forget a mother talking about her son at an Al-Anon meeting that I had attended. For years, she had allowed her son to live with her, and she took care of him while he wasted his life away using one drug after another. It was her turn to talk. She had long, stringy gray hair and dark circles under her tired eyes, filled with deep wrinkles showing the strain that this mothering-a-drug-addict life had put on her.

She began talking as she rubbed her bony fingers with the palms of her age-spotted hands. "I don't know. I think it's too late. I think my son is a vegetable now ... He's been using for so long. I'm afraid that if I kick my son out, he will just die on the streets." She continued to treat her addicted son as if he were still her son and nothing was different, except that he was now using heroin, meth, cocaine, whatever he could get a high from. She didn't want to see that a monster had taken over her son, and yet she felt that he was not really there anymore. In reality, her son was there, just so small inside his body as the monster of heroin or other DOC (drug of choice) had taken over, and she did nothing but make the monster comfortable. She allowed the monster to stay and grow. And grow it did ... bigger and stronger until her son was barely there ...

My thoughts were to always love my son but to support him only if he was in recovery. If he was using, I would not support him. He could not live in my house, eat my food, enjoy a roof over his head, or have a warm bed to sleep in if he was using. I'd love him no matter what, but I would not help him in anyway if he was using—if he had the monster inhabiting his body. I knew I had to be mean to the monster. I had to make that monster miserable and want to get out. Yes, I had to take the chance that the monster may self-harm or kill the body it was inhabiting, but wasn't it doing that anyway?

The monster would yell and scream and threaten to never love me again. As long as he was using, he was the monster. The monster would do anything to get what it wanted. The monster would become a master manipulator, liar, and thief.

I read the hundreds of stories and books and blogs—parents practically killing themselves to help their addicted children, spouses giving everything to help their addicted spouses, but who were they really helping? The monster. You can't love the monster. You must be mean to the monster, make the strict rules and stick to them, and take the monster to real specialists for help—specialists who will take blood samples or hair samples for drug tests, knowing the monster will buy clean urine and hide it in or on places of their bodies to keep it warm for your store-bought drug tests. By telling the monster that if it wanted to live under my roof it had to do everything I said and do it how I said it needed to be done or the monster could find another place to live, I wasn't being mean to my son; I was loving my son. I was doing everything I could to pull my son up from the depths of nowhere-but-heroin land and back into his body.

I had a friend, Patty, who lived in the same neighborhood and had children the same age as mine. Our youngest daughters were in the same kindergarten class and became friends, which is how we met. Her older daughter, Kathy, was a year older than Elliott and also became addicted to heroin. Kathy was a beautiful intelligent girl who was in the same Running Start program that Elliott was involved in and graduated from high school with her associate of arts degree. She was awarded an academic scholarship to a city college in Denver. The heroin caught up to her during her first year, and she dropped out.

Patty kicked Kathy out of the house for a week. Kathy was walking the streets when Patty saw her and couldn't stand it. Patty invited Kathy back in her house and allowed her and her drug-dealing boyfriend to live in the basement of her new $900,000 home. Neither Kathy nor her boyfriend worked. They just lived in the basement, both high as a kite. Patty was humiliated and didn't want to talk about it, but I asked her about Kathy one day. Patty knew what I went through with Elliott and trusted me and valued my advice. Patty told me she couldn't bear to see her baby girl walking the streets selling her body for a high. She didn't want to be a part of her demise and have to one day identify her daughter's body in a morgue. With her logic, she was on her way to discovering her daughter's dead body in her basement. A year later, her heroin-addicted daughter was pregnant.

It sounds like I had everything to do with Elliott's recovery. I didn't. But I didn't stop, and I found doctors who knew how to deal with adolescent addiction and could turn me to resources that could help me help him. It really does take a village, but sometimes you have to build the village yourself.

Forty-one

May and Summer of 2013 - Zumiez

WHEN ELLIOTT CAME HOME FROM MOUNTAIN WEST BEHAVIORAL, HE TOLD US that he didn't want to be sharing homes and going back and forth. He wanted to stay in one place, and he chose my house over his dad's apartment. With the same logic from the first rehabilitation to change the environment so Elliott would not have memories of using heroin, which may trigger a craving, we moved his bedroom into the family room this time. I refused to give up my room again.

The family room was a long room added onto my 1950s home that was attached to the kitchen. When the addition was constructed, the door in the kitchen that led to the backyard was removed, which left a doorway into the family room, now Elliott's bedroom.

The room was long and had two doors that led outside, one to the side patio and the other to the backyard. It had dark paneling and an old wood stove. It was always cooler than the rest of the house temperature wise, but that dark paneling did *not* make it cool in any other way. The insulation was lacking, which created the cooler temperatures, and there must have been cracks in places, as there seemed to be a lot more spiders in the family room than in any other room. The sacrifices one makes to stay clean from heroin. A bigger room with more spiders is a good exchange for memories of smoking heroin and barfing in the wastebasket.

We moved Elliott's bed and dresser to the family room and the couch and television to his old room. He wanted me to install a door between the kitchen and his new bedroom for privacy, but I never got around to it. The room was long enough that his bed could not be seen from the kitchen doorway, so that was private enough for me. Elliott was lucky; he got the biggest room in the house. I didn't mind using his small bedroom for the television room. If it was helping Elliott have a new surrounding with no memories of smoking heroin like the other bedrooms and was going to help him stay clean, that's all I cared about. *Support the measures being taken to stay clean* was what I kept hearing in the back of my mind.

Elliott worked hard those first few weeks. He went to meetings twice a day. He kept himself busy staying in touch with friends he'd made at Mountain West Behavioral and looking for a job. His high school required a senior project, which was started when he was a sophomore. He had the project completed, but his adviser told him he still needed the form that showed where he obtained the information in his project. Elliott believed he had already given it to his adviser and was unable to find it. He was missing language credits, and his senior project was not considered complete. He was not going to graduate with his class.

I took him to a school that specializes in unique situations, usually those situations were dealing with extreme athletes who traveled for their sports, but this was still unique in its own way. Elliott and I went to the school and spoke with the owner. We officially pulled him out of his previous high school enrollment and had his transcripts sent to the specialized school. They created a plan for Elliott to take classes to fulfill the high school graduation requirements. I shelled out more money. *Let's get you back on track, Elliott*, I thought. *Let's get you back to life where you can be successful.*

Elliott found a job at a popular retail clothing/skateboarding/snowboarding store called Zumiez. Turned out, a manager of one of the stores was also in recovery and spotted Elliott at an AA meeting. She asked him if he needed work and would be interested in working at her store. Working at Zumiez for Elliott would be like working for Nordstrom's for a teenage girl ... heaven. Zumiez was in a mall and where the cool kids went to get their expensive clothes, skateboards, snowboards, and related gear. Elliott never thought of himself as a cool kid, so to be working at Zumiez and selling their products to the hip kids who came in with their wealthy parents who would drop fifty times what was in his bank account was exhilarating for him.

Soon, Elliott was top salesman, working double shifts and going to daily meetings. He stopped all schoolwork. Who had that kind of time? Was I disappointed? Oh, hail yes I was, but he was staying clean, and that's all I cared about.

Do whatever it takes to stay clean. Keep up the good work, Elliott. You've got this, Elliott! I was his biggest fan if he was clean. I was his loudest cheerleader. And he did. He was succeeding at staying clean. He was succeeding at being the charming top salesman at Zumiez, outselling all other sales coworkers. And he was succeeding at charming the pants off the girls ... literally.

Elliott had a plethora of girls basically throwing themselves at him both at Zumiez and AA meetings. I was meeting new girls every few days—all of them beautiful. They would shake my hand when Elliott introduced them to me and look at me in a I-hope-you-like-me-because-I-like-your-son kind of way. Those pleading pretty eyes, as if I could have anything to do with them having a lasting relationship with my son. I saw hardly any of them twice.

It was all fine and dandy until I found little "gifts" on the floor of his new bedroom.

In order to get to my backyard to take a hot tub soak, I had to walk past his bed. One evening just before going to bed, I put on my bathrobe and slippers and was walking through his room, and there it was—a crumpled-up, used condom. This thought kept creeping up in the back of my mind: Was Elliott using sex to replace his addiction to heroin? Surprisingly enough, I was OK with that. As long as sex was consensual and he was using protection, then for the time I was fine. Did it bother me that he was bringing home strangers and having sex with them under my roof? Yes, but my imminent desire was for Elliott to stay clean from heroin.

When I found this special gift, for lack of a better word, Elliott was at a meeting, so I took a picture of the used condom on the floor and sent it to him. I asked him to clean up the room he was staying in and to throw any and all used condoms in the wastebasket provided to him next to his dresser. He apologized and told me he would do better. What more could a mother ask for?

Forty-two

Autumn 2013 to Spring 2014 - Get Away from Colorado and Bounce Right Back

ELLIOTT WAS GETTING RECOGNITION FOR HIS HARD WORK AT ZUMIEZ. HE WON a trip to Vail, Colorado, where all of the top salesmen and saleswomen were taken to spend a long weekend skiing, hiking, and hanging out together. The reward was appreciated, but Elliott was struggling with staying in Loveland. He found that the NA (Narcotics Anonymous) meetings were a great hangout for drug dealers and stopped going. Instead, he went to AA meetings and found them to be more in line with what he needed. He was getting restless and wanted to join his older brother, Brandon, who was bartending in Austin, Texas, and trying to make a go at a music career.

Brandon got his first guitar when he was in third grade and had been part of a band ever since. Eventually, he actually had a real band with a drummer and other musicians. He even got a few gigs in bars in Aurora. I always thought Denver was the best place to be, but according to Brandon, it was Austin where SXSW (South by Southwest) festival was held. *That* was the place to be discovered.

Elliott decided on a whim that he wanted to go spend time with Brandon in Austin, Texas. So, he quit his job at Zumiez and took a bus down to Texas. It all happened so fast. One minute he was top salesman at a huge retail store, and the next he was looking for a job in Texas. It was back to me and Melissa. I'm not really sure what happened that led Elliott to make this move, but in less than a year, he came back.

Nine months after moving to Austin, Elliott called me from a bar that he was working at, and I could tell from the tone of his voice that he was down. Before this, we spoke on almost a weekly basis. He found a job at a bar with Brandon and was making his rent and paying his bills, but something wasn't right for him. He told me that most of his friends were Brandon's age, and he didn't feel like he really fit in. He also told me he didn't want his life to be working at a bar like those so-called friends were doing. He wanted more; he knew he needed to go back to school. There's not a lot available for high school dropouts. He asked if he could come home. Of course he could. Within days, he was back in Colorado and looking up ways he could get his high school diploma. He didn't want a GED; that would not be a reflection of his intelligence.

Aims Community College, where he was on the presidential honor roll during his Running Start experience, was his saving grace. They offered a program where Elliott could take the necessary classes with them to get his high school diploma and college credit. Elliott started going back to school.

Charming the pants off the girls didn't stop, though. I had rearranged the rooms to take over the family room as my television relaxation room and told Elliott that he could stay with me, but he would have to stay in his old room. I asked if he was OK with that, and he was. By then, he was two years clean, and he told me he didn't ever want to do hard drugs again. He did want to try social drinking, though, so against my advice, he would crack open a beer every once in a while. He was over the legal drinking age, so he wasn't illegal, but in the back of my mind, I was concerned.

He brought home a girl one night. There was something about her that I didn't like. I also didn't want my life to be back to where it had been a year earlier, letting Elliott do basically anything he wanted so long as he stayed clean from heroin. I needed to lay down some boundaries and rules, and this girl made me decide to do it hard. They went into his room and shut the door. Nope, I didn't like that. I knew what was going to happen, and I was shaking my head back and forth, saying, "Nope, nope, not this again." I knocked on his door and asked him if I could talk to him. Elliott came out, and I told him that I didn't want him bringing strange girls home and sleeping with them in my home. I didn't mind it if he was in a relationship with someone and I had gotten to know her, but I refused to have my home be a whore hotel. Elliott wasn't paying rent, as he was going to school, so my house, my rules.

He understood and said they were just leaving. They walked out the front door, and I locked it as I was going to bed. I assumed the two of them were going out somewhere and Elliott had his house key. Elliott was only walking this yucky girl to her car and completely misunderstood my locking the front door as a sign that I was locking him out and didn't want him there anymore. Elliott was mad and left with her. She must have taken him to his dads because that's where he said he was going when I saw him the next day. I was OK with that plan. Maybe his dad would allow strange girls to come over and Elliott could have more freedom, so I didn't argue.

Elliott misinterpreted that too. He was a sensitive young man and not very secure with himself. For weeks, I could feel a heavy and sad aura around him. I asked him what was going on, and he barfed out his feelings about how I hurt him when I locked the front door and how I didn't care that he went to live with his dad. My floor dropped out from under me. I felt like such a crappy mother. How could I do such a thing? I wrapped my arms around him and apologized and told him my version of what happened. It's amazing how a simple activity can be interpreted completely different from one person to another. I told Elliott that he was welcome to come stay and/or live with me anytime, and I had not intended to lock him out like he thought. Elliott was OK to just continue living with Blake; the room in his apartment was bigger and brighter than the bedroom in my small house, and he needed that.

Blake had moved to a large townhome that he was renting. It had three large bedrooms with vaulted ceilings and large windows. A few months later, when Melissa was in her winter quarter of her senior year of high school and heavily involved with the drama department, Blake decided to move to a swank two-bedroom apartment in Denver. "Sorry, Melissa, no bedroom for you, but you can come visit and sleep in my bed, and I'll take the couch." Those were Blake's comments to his seventeen-year-old daughter when he moved a good hour or more drive away from her and for the first time didn't have a bedroom for her.

Forty-three

Spring to Summer 2017 - Grandpa Duck

MY OLDEST SISTER'S FIRSTBORN WAS GETTING MARRIED, THE FIRST WEDDING from my nuclear family, and we were all invited. Dria wanted the entire family involved and asked Melissa to be one of her bridesmaids. Initially, Melissa excitedly agreed but had to later decline when she won a star role in her high school musical, which was performing the play the weekend of the wedding. So, it was just Nick and I and the boys, Elliott and Brandon, going to the wedding.

Elliott was back in Loveland taking classes at Aims Community College. He got his high school diploma and had about a year of college under his belt. He was on the presidential honor roll again. To this day I still remember him telling me during his time in the first rehab center that he got on the presidential honor roll because of the heroin and that he did so well on stage because of the heroin. An addict thinks it's the drug that makes him succeed … It's not.

Elliott was nervous about going back to Nevada for the wedding. He felt branded as the heroin addict of the family. He hardly knew my nuclear family, and he had trepidations of what this short trip would be like. His insecurities swelled, but we were meeting up with Brandon who was flying in from Texas, and Elliott knew Brandon would be right there by his side to protect him from any of the feared snide remarks or judgmental looks from cousins, aunts, or uncles.

There were no snide remarks or judgmental looks. My family was warm and accepting. We all had our issues, and they knew it. One cousin almost OD'd trying an experimental drug for the first time, another cousin used food to wallow her troubles in and was a hundred pounds overweight, and another cousin had his mother, my sister, find emails he was going to send to all of his family members after he killed himself. Of course, that didn't happen, but we all had our disfunctions, and my family knew that Elliott's heroin addiction was no different. Perfect families, perfect lives … They don't exist. We are all just doing the best we can.

We refer to my dad as Grandpa Duck. Why that name? He was a very sarcastic, funny little man. I don't mean funny like strange but funny like always making people laugh. He had this way of looking at you with his brown eyes and a smirk on his wrinkly face as he called you a duck for one reason or another. You knew right then and there that he was trying to make you laugh, which meant he loved you. Elliott and Brandon hung out with Grandpa Duck at the wedding for a little while. I looked over at them after the wedding ceremony and before the reception. Two young men and my little old dad were laughing about something—I don't know what.

A few days later, Grandpa Duck and I were talking in the car, and he got really serious. He had just parked the car and paused for a moment. Then he looked at me and told me that he was concerned about Brandon. He didn't seem to know what he was doing with his life or where he was going. Brandon was my artist and musician; he will find his way in life but not the typical way. I wasn't worried. Then my dad said to me, "I'm really impressed with Elliott. Elliott is going somewhere. He's got his head on right. You tell him that, Karen. You tell him that I said that, all right?" I told him I would.

Two months later, Nick proposed and told me that when we were out to Nevada for the wedding, he and my dad played a round of golf, and he'd asked Grandpa Duck for permission to marry me. Grandpa Duck broke down and cried right there on the golf course. The crying was his relief that I'd finally found a good man. He gave Nick his approval and blessing and then got a birdie on the next hole. Nick told G Duck that he had to give me away at our wedding. G Duck died about a month after our engagement, but he made it to the wedding … He was there. I felt him.

After G Duck died, a friend and I were shopping about a half-hour drive away from Nick's cabin where we were staying for the weekend. My friend and I had stopped at a few shops on the quaint main street, and it was time for a rest. We walked into an open concept restaurant/bar that was full of beautiful people in their twenties and thirties who were casually socializing and sat down at the bar for a drink and a bite to eat. I had just placed my bags and purse down by my feet when my dad's favorite Frank Sinatra song, "My Way," came on the speakers. My sisters and I chose this song and several others to play during a slideshow that we put together and played during my dad's celebration of life service. When I heard this song come on after a string of hipster songs, I thought about how strange it was for this restaurant/bar to change gears like that and play this song. I got all teary-eyed hearing it. It made me think of my dad, the G Duck. But I composed myself and wiped away the tears from my eyes. I didn't want to make my friend uncomfortable. She was actually Nick's best friend's wife, and I didn't know her well enough to break down.

A few nights later, Nick and I and his best friend and wife were out to a completely different restaurant, and the same song came on … Again, the tears started swelling up, and the lump in my throat started choking me. That's when I knew it was my dad; he was letting me know he was there. He never made it to that part of the country, but I had begged for him to come visit, come play golf with Nick, come up and go fishing off the dock. He never made it up, at least not when he was inhabiting his human body. His spirit was there, and he made sure I knew it.

At my wedding, I had the song picked out for my daddy-daughter dance, which I never had before and never will. I wished that my dad, G Duck, would show himself at our wedding, but I wasn't going to take the chance that he wouldn't, so I planned the dance to be with my sons. Just as the reception started and everyone was sitting down for the dinner, the DJ started playing random songs that I hadn't given him. "What a Wonderful World" by Louis Armstrong came on … I was shocked. G Duck was there. My mom, myself, and my two sisters all looked at each other, and we all knew.

Forty-four

August 2017 - Empty Nest for One Month

Nick had lived with Melissa and me for a year during her senior year of high school when she had chosen to attend Colorado State University. She graduated from high school and was on her way to CSU. Elliott was living with his dad, Blake, in Denver and loving the environment. He found a great AA meeting group close to his apartment. He was waiting tables at a hipster restaurant and dating a sweet and pretty blonde girl who was the hostess—the hostess with the mostest.

Melissa moved out of the house and into her college dorms in August. I drove down with her. Blake and his mother followed us. Unfortunately, a block into the drive my car started showing signs of problems, so we turned around and unloaded Melissa's stuff from my car and piled it into Blake's mom's car. Thank God for moms! This meant I was stuck with Blake and his mom for the entire time, though, which was not something I was looking forward to. *Do it for Melissa,* I told myself. *It is not every day your baby girl moves into her college dorm for the first time. We can all get along and enjoy this experience. It is just a few hours.*

It was a whole day of waiting in lines, moving her stuff in when it was our turn, and then saying goodbye before trekking back home. Poor Blake was afraid he would fall asleep while driving, so his mommy drove his car, and I drove hers, which was fine, as it kept them together and me by myself to listen to music and my thoughts. We made a stop to eat dinner at a gas station/convenience store where a Subway restaurant was built in. The three of us gassed up our cars and went inside to order a sandwich and eat. Blake got a few candy bars and immediately started complaining about his fears of being fired.

Having heard this a million times in our marriage, I spoke up. "You are always afraid of losing your jobs, and you never do." I couldn't help myself. It just flew out of my mouth without any hesitation like it had been there dying to get out for years.

Silence. Both Blake and his mother looked up at me, stunned that I would say such a thing.

I just looked back at them and shrugged my shoulders. "It's true, Blake. You have *always* had the fear of being fired, but you never get fired. Get over it, and just give them your best ..."

To my surprise, Blake and his mother both agreed. But how could they not? It was true. Sometimes the truth just needs to be said. It needs to be put out there for all to see and accept. Stop putting your head in the sand and pretending the obvious isn't there or it's something else. Open your eyes, and see what's really in front of you, whether it's your irrational fears or the fact that your son is a heroin addict. The skill is to be able to step back and see what's really in front of you. For Blake, it was his extreme anxiety, irrational fears, and self-centeredness that was so consuming he could hardly function. For David, it was his heroin-addicted son who was not helping himself and supposedly keeping his addiction under control by purchasing Suboxone on the street and treating his addiction problem by himself without the need for doctors. For Patty, it was her daughter, Kathy's, heroin addiction that was getting worse as she continued to allow Kathy and her drug-dealing boyfriend to live in her basement and now start a family that Patty would most likely be raising.

Reality and truth can be difficult to look at, but we all have difficulty with it to one degree or another. If you continue to sweep problems under the rug or stick your head in the sand and hope the problem goes away on its own, then you are part of the problem itself. It takes courage and strength to pull your head out of the sand—or anywhere else it may be—and truly look at what is going on around you, whether it's to yourself or a loved one. Look at the problem for what it is, and you'll be taking the first step to being part of the answer.

Nick and I had the whole house to ourselves. It was glorious. It didn't last, though, because Elliott moved back in September. Blake told Elliott he was going to rent a room in a house, and he would need to find another place to live. And that brings us full circle in my story.

Forty-five

Spring/Summer 2018 - Acceptance

It was now spring of 2018. Elliott was on his medication and was seeing my therapist, Michael Ross, twice a month. He had almost two years of college under his belt and was talking about wanting to experience a university. Aims Community College offered Running Start, so it was inundated with high school students taking college courses and was a small campus. Elliott wanted the adult college; he wanted to experience a real university.

Nick and Elliott had bonded. Nick had his own history and was able to use his life experiences to help Elliott with his suicide ideations and depression. Nick woke up early every morning and went to the gym to work out. He got to his law office early and was working before most people finish their breakfast. Positivity oozed out of him. It was so refreshing to be with someone who took the bull by the horns and rode it through. Problems were challenges to be conquered in his eyes. Nothing was too big to handle. Nick was calm and even-keeled. He took care of everyone and listened endlessly. He was so different from Blake, and I was so happy.

Nick rubbed off on Elliott. Nick was a real man who didn't need his wife to be his mommy and take care of him. He and Elliott would cook dinner together and talk. A person couldn't help but become motivated being around Nick. Anything was possible; you just had to work harder than anyone else if you wanted it bad enough. Nothing was just dropped in your lap; you had to earn it.

Something transformed in Elliott by having just this little bit of time around Nick. Elliott realized that he could do anything. He just needed to work harder and reach for what he wanted. Elliott sent one application to the university of his dreams. He didn't tell me right away which university it was. *Please let it be close*, was all I thought. He put all his eggs in one basket and refused to make a plan B. Sometimes his anxiety would creep back in, and he would make the old negative comments about not being accepted and not knowing what he would do when the rejection letter came in.

The letter came, but it wasn't a rejection. Elliott was accepted to Cornell University. We were in the kitchen, and he already knew but told me in a very nonchalant way. "Yeah, Mom. I'll be going to Cornell University next year, so uh …"

I shook my head as if that would help me hear him better and leaned in closer to him. "What? What did you say? Where are you going?"

Elliott had the acceptance letter in his hand behind his back and pulled it out to show me. "I got accepted to Cornell University—the Ivy League university in New York."

"Are you kidding me? You got in? Oh my God! Oh my God!" I hugged that slender boy so hard with tears streaming down my face. It all came rushing back to me in that very moment. Finding the heroin, taking him to rehab only to have him relapse shortly after Christmas, watching him throw up in his wastebasket, visiting him at Mountain West Behavioral, seeing him struggle to get a 4.0 at Aims Community College as he got his high school diploma, and watching him get to two years underneath him. This couldn't be real, but it was—my Elliott had been accepted to an Ivy League university, and just five years earlier he'd been a heroin-addicted high school dropout. I pulled back from the huge hug and looked at him. His face was flushed, and his big blue eyes were watering.

"I'm so proud of you, Elliott."

And he just replied, "Thanks, Mom. I couldn't have done it without you."

I had a dentist appointment that I realized I was running late to, so I kissed my Elliott on the cheek and told him I had to run to the dentist and ran out of the house happy as a clam. I drove to the dentist just a few blocks away and ran into the office. They brought me back to the treatment room, and I couldn't help but share the news with my dentist and his darling assistant of five years who knew Elliott. As I was telling them about Elliott's acceptance, I heard the song "What a Wonderful World" start playing in the background. Grandpa Duck was there letting me know he was aware of what was happening, and I broke down and cried right there in the dentist chair.

Forty-six

Summer 2018 - $80,000 to Attend

A FEW DAYS AFTER THE EXCITEMENT AND THRILL OF ELLIOTT'S ACCEPTANCE passed, the real work began. How was Elliott going to afford to go to Cornell University? The website listed a cost of $80,000 a year to attend. Elliott started applying for student loans. Blake was making almost $250,000 a year, well more than double my salary, so I told Elliott to ask Blake to cosign for a student loan. We all knew Blake would not *give* Elliott any money, but maybe, just maybe, he would give him a signature. A signature would allow Elliott to attend Cornell University. Elliott agreed to ask him.

I returned from work a few days later, and Elliott was sitting on the concrete entry steps to the front door. I could faintly hear Elliott crying. I had parked my car on the street. I was walking up to the house and could see him with his head down in his arms, which were leaning on his bent knees, and he was shaking with sobs. What had happened? How could such an exciting, happy time turn around so quickly? I ran up to him and asked him what was wrong. I leaned over him and put my hands on his shoulders before squatting down and looking up at his face as he lifted his head. Snot was running out of his nose as he wiped it on his sleeve. His eyes were red, and his face was blotched and wet from his tears.

"I can't go. I can't go, Mom. Dad won't cosign for a loan. He says he doesn't agree with my screenwriting major, so he won't cosign. I've called every student loan company, and none of them will give me a loan without a cosigner."

Blake … How could he pull something like this? Blake always wanted to go to medical school and be a doctor, but his MD father didn't agree. Blake suffered throughout his adult life with regret for not following his dreams and listening to his father's advice instead. Now he was deciding to do the same to his own son—unbelievable.

That morning, unbeknownst to Elliot, I had applied to my credit union for a home equity line of credit (HLOC) and was accepted within hours. "Elliott, you are going to Cornell. I'm going to help you get there." I told him about getting accepted for a HLOC that day and that I did it as a precautionary measure in case anything else didn't work out. It was my Elliott's Cornell University insurance policy. Thank God housing values were skyrocketing. There was no way I was going to let my son work so hard to get clean from heroin, return to school to get his high school diploma, and *not* go to the university of his dreams. Elliott was going to Cornell University.

In his first year at Cornell, Elliott made the dean's list. That summer Elliott got a job with his brother, Brandon, who had also moved to New York for career opportunities of his own. I can't help but think about the lyrics to a song my father loved by Frank Sinatra: "If you can make it there, you'll make it anywhere." Although my two boys were there for different reasons, this was a true test for both of them.

The job Elliott started that summer was in a bar as a barback, and Brandon worked as the bartender. This bar wasn't your typical sports bar with a hundred different choices of beer and peanuts in a bowl at every table. This was one of those New York City specialty bars where the male staff would wear nice black pants with a white shirt and fancy tie. High-paid attorneys would frequent this bar and leave my boys tips that could pay for a nice dinner in Denver, Colorado.

The bar staff were known to occasionally have a drink with the patrons and toast to their next endeavor or upcoming trial they were leading. The owner of the bar thought it would create bonding with the patrons and keep them coming back. That may have been the best thing for the bar owner and patrons, but it wasn't the best thing for a recovering addict.

The words from the doctor who we first took Elliott to when we discovered his heroin addiction would ring true. Once an addict, always an addict. "This will be a struggle for you during your entire life, Elliott."

A few months after Elliott began working at the bar, he began his second year at Cornell and realized he was having trouble with alcohol. He called me in tears. "Mom, I can't do it. I have a drinking problem. I think I might have to drop out and come home."

"Elliott, get help. I'm sure Cornell has counselors who can get you into a program that could help you. If you need to come home, you are welcome to, but first, find out if you can get some kind of medical leave and come back when you are ready," was my reply.

Elliott's insecurities came flowing out, and he began to sob. I wanted to crawl inside my phone, shoot myself through the telephone wires to him, and wrap my arms around him. I was literally on the other side of the nation and unable to do anything but use my words. I let him cry and tried comforting him. "It's going to be all right, Elliott. You are on the dean's list. Cornell knows how hard you are working. They will help you. They want you to succeed."

The comfort then stopped, and I spoke some truth. Sometimes a momma has to say it like it is—tough love—or her baby won't grow and move forward. "Elliott, I'm proud of you for realizing that you can't drink casually. Some people don't realize this until they have ruined their lives and the lives around them. So realizing this in only a few months is quite an accomplishment. But you are going to continue to struggle and find yourself here over and over again until you truly dig deep—and I mean to the day when your life changed. The day you went next door and lost your trust in others. Promise me, Elliott, that when you get help, you will work through that event."

The other line was silent for a while, and then I heard, "I will, Mom. I promise."

Elliott found help and signed up for an outpatient rehabilitation program where he participated in group sessions and private therapy. He took a leave for that semester but was able to return to Cornell and continued getting his As.

At the time of this final chapter, my Elliott is still in Cornell, getting As, and projecting to graduate in a year and a half. His dream is to write scripts for *Saturday Night Live*, create Broadway shows, and become a great stand-up comic. I told him to dream big now—it's his time. My dream for him is that he conquers his fears and insecurities and finds happiness—and, of course, stays clean and sober.

Printed in the United States
by Baker & Taylor Publisher Services